Reading the Map:
"Lessons from the Book of Genesis"
Volume Two

Reading the Map
Lessons from the Book of Genesis
(Volume Two)

Preface

Faith is the ability to see life through "God glasses". Biblically speaking it is the choice to look at life through the lens of God's Word – the Bible. Probably no other person in the Bible is such an exemplar of the concept of a "faith walk" as Abraham, the father of the Hebrew people. His life journey is what the section of Genesis 11-25 is chiefly about – and these lessons follow the course through those chapters of Genesis. In lessons 10-25 of the series, we will see the "faith exchange" defined, and follow Abraham through his life "searching for a city whose architect and builder was God." (Hebrews 11:10).

Our studies begin by a fire and a simple story of a needlepoint tapestry – and end with the lessons of life learned as an ancient grieving family gathered to bury their Patriarch. This is the story of a man called by God – but it is much more. It is the story of a dynasty begun by a couple that lives on in a people today. While very important, both Abraham and his wife were presented in an utterly flawed "warts and all" portrait in the Bible – and our lessons will carefully show how God used them in spite of their frailties.

Lessons in Volume Two

Lesson Sixteen: Gen 17:1-16 "The Terms of God's Blessing" (pp. 77-87)

> Key Principle: An open heart to revealed truth leads to solid beliefs and obedient steps. These lead to fulfillment of one's deepest longings and desires.

Lesson Seventeen: Genesis 17-18 "The Mother of All Blessing" (pp. 89-100)

> Key Principle: My surrender to God as a mom is vital to the blessing of my family, and the future of my heritage.

Lesson Eighteen:" Genesis 18:16-19:38 "Choosing My Stage" (101-114)

> Key Principle: Godliness isn't only about how I act; it is about where I choose to place myself.

Lesson Nineteen: Genesis 20 "Connecting the Dots" (pp. 115-125)

> Key Principle: I need to connect the daily choices I make to the purposes God has set forth in His Word for me.

Lesson Twenty: Genesis 21:1-21 "Encore for a Villain" (pp. 127-137)

> Key Principle: God may bring back a long ago problem to strip me down – but He will use it to direct me to my proper place and unfold His promises to me!

Lesson Twenty-one: Genesis 21:22-34 "Seven Character Traits of Maturity" (pp. 139-150)

> Key Principle: The character traits of a mature believer are measurable and defined.

Lesson Twenty-two: Genesis 22 "The Grand Prize for the Great Surrender" (pp. 151-163)

Key Principle: When a believer surrenders completely to God, God fills his life with the greatest provision of all – Himself. It is an existence more satisfying than any other.

Lesson Twenty-three: Genesis 23 "Five Lessons from Painful Loss" (pp. 165-174)

Key Principle: Loss in this life is part of God's training ground for all of us.

Lesson Twenty-four: Genesis 24 "A Family Affair" (pp. 175-185)

Key Principle: God defines the family and God reveals how it should work.

Lesson Twenty-five: Genesis 25 "Lessons from the Family Tree" (pp. 187-198)

Key Principle: The family was intended to be God's learning laboratory

Reading the Map:
Lessons in Genesis

Lesson Ten: Genesis 11:10-12:8
"A Story in the Tapestry"

Carl was curled up on the braided rug, only feet from the crackling fire that warmed the whole end of the house. He sat quietly for a long time watching the quick and succinct movements of his mother's fingers as she sewed the cloth that hung from her lap to the floor. After a long while, gazing at her work, the puzzled look on his face became an unsettling stare, and his mother wanted to know where his mind was traveling.

"Darling, what is the matter?" Carl hesitated, searching for words. He frowned and said, "Mommy, that is the ugliest thing I have ever seen!" Realizing his position on the floor, his mother turned her tapestry over to see the back – the part he was staring at. Carl was right! It was ugly – full of hanging threads and long knots, string and thread was crossed in various ways and made no sense!

Mom replied, "Oh Sweetie, you are right, but you are looking at it all wrong! From the side you see you cannot see what I am making. The story can only make sense from this side. If you look at it from up here, it is beautiful!" With that she turned the tapestry over for him to see. It WAS flat, colorful and... well, beautiful. Every stitch made sense.

Carl saw it and said, "OH Mom! It is PERFECT! I couldn't see what you saw!"

The truth is, that is life is for us on Earth. **We see the dangling threads; they crossed strings and from our very limited human perspective we try to make sense of life** – but often we just can't this side of glory. Even though that is the case, for the believer, he or she gets a **glimpse** of how GOD is weaving the tapestry of our lives from up above, and the Word opens a glimpse of HIS perspective – because only from above can the right side of that tapestry be truly displayed.

Key Principle: God's story will become clearer in my life if I look at things from His side of the tapestry.

In our text for this lesson, we can see **eight features of our life** that have been woven to tell our story. As we look across each, we will see the grand workmanship of an artistic master:

Feature One: Life's confusion swallowed you up and you didn't feel like you were anyone of significance or special importance (Gen. 11:1-9).

Let's face it. The world is a big place in many ways. I am one of six billion people. Every second five people are born and two people die, a net gain of three people... It took about forty years for the population to nearly double in the end of the twentieth century because of advancement in medical care. Each of the six billion people has their own hopes and dreams. I am just one of the many.

Genesis 10:1-5 tells of a whole group of humanity that moved from the Shinar plain to what is now **Europe and Russia**.

Genesis 10:1 "Now the whole earth used the same language and the same words. 2 It came about as they journeyed east, that they found a plain in the land of Shinar and settled there. 3 They said to one another, "Come, let us make bricks and burn [them] thoroughly." And they used brick for stone, and they used tar for mortar. 4 They said, "Come, let us build for ourselves a city, and a tower whose top [will reach] into heaven, and let us make for ourselves a name, otherwise we will be scattered abroad over the face of the whole earth." 5 The LORD came down to see the city and the tower which the sons of men had built."

They got there because God separated their language stems and they gathered together in places where they could understand each other. Their bodies adapted to the environment, as did their languages. People in cold regions developed many words for types of snow, but only one for sand.

This adaptation does not prove evolution – quite the opposite. Brad Harrub, Ph.D., Bert Thompson, Ph.D., and Dave Miller, Ph.D.in <u>The Origin of Language and Communication</u>, published in 2003 says: "The most ancient languages for which we have written texts are often far more intricate and complicated in their grammatical forms than many contemporary languages."

Also, consider that when language first appears on the scene, it already is fully developed and very complex. The late Harvard paleontologist George Gaylord Simpson described it this way: "Even the peoples with least complex cultures have highly sophisticated languages, with complex grammar and large vocabularies, capable of naming and discussing anything that occurs in the sphere occupied by their speakers. The oldest language that can be reconstructed is already modern, sophisticated, and complete from an evolutionary point of view."

Chomsky summed it up well when he stated: "Human language appears to be a unique phenomenon, without significant analogue in the animal world ... There is no reason to suppose that the 'gaps' are bridgeable. There is no more of a basis for assuming an evolutionary development from breathing to walking."

Genesis 10:6-20 tells us of the **African** dispersion. Genesis 10:21-32 explains the **Near and Far Eastern** dispersion of linguistic groups.

Look at the beginning of the passage in Genesis 11:6: *"The LORD said, "Behold, they are one people, and they all have the same language. And this is what they began to do, and now nothing which they purpose to do will be impossible for them. 7"Come, let Us go down and there confuse their language, so that they will not understand one another's speech." 8So the LORD scattered them abroad from there over the face of the whole earth; and they stopped building the city. 9Therefore its name was called Babel, because there the LORD confused the language of the whole earth; and from there the LORD scattered them abroad over the face of the whole earth."*

It is clear the Biblical formula for the division of the nations was God's idea. Men together meant men scheming deeper rebellion. God stepped in, and now we are one in billions- separated by language, culture and developmental history. With all the people on earth…perhaps in the litany of people of Earth you came to God when you didn't feel particularly special. That's understandable. In fact, it's likely that you were… well…average. The problem is, that isn't God's view – and His is the **TRUTH**. **We believe LIES about God and ourselves!**

Listen to what He sees in you:

- **Lie: "God doesn't know me!"**
- **Truth: I am *intimately* known**.

Psalm 139:1 O LORD, You have searched (chawkar:examined) me and known (yadah: experienced) me.

- **Lie: "God knows only the big and important things!"**
- **Truth: He knows every mundane part of my life!**

Psalm 139:2 You know when I sit down and when I rise up (my mundane movements).

- **Lie: "God is too removed to understand me!"**
- **Truth: He totally and completely examines and comprehends your motives and actions**.

Psalm 139:2b: You understand my thought from afar (rawchoke: a distance away). 3 You scrutinize (zerita from the word to winnow or scatter – zawraw) my path and my lying down, and are intimately acquainted (sawkan: intimately aware of) with all my ways.

- **Lie: "God is taken by surprise at my 'spontaneity!'"**
- **Truth: He knew before you did!**

Psalm 139:4 Even before there is a word on my tongue, behold, O LORD, You know it all.

- **Lie: "I just got here – no plan, no purpose!"**
- **Truth: I had a guide blocking for me all the way!**

Reading the Map: Lessons in Genesis

Psalm 139:5 You have enclosed me behind and before, and laid Your hand upon me. 6 Such knowledge is too wonderful for me; It is too high, I cannot attain to it.

The Biblical truth is that there is no coincidence or happenstance in your life. God has been at work the whole time. He knows it all – even before we do. He understands it all better than I can. I may seem small, but He knows my name! I am called His friend, His beloved and His treasure. I am neither small nor insignificant based on the precious price He paid for me.

*Peter 1:17b …Conduct yourselves in fear during the time of your stay on Earth; 18 knowing that you were **not redeemed with perishable things** like silver or gold from your futile way of life inherited from your forefathers, 19 **but with precious blood**, as of a lamb unblemished and spotless, the blood of Christ.*

Feature Two: God targeted your life long before you knew anything about Him – long before you were even born (Gen. 11:10-26).

Look at the verses between Genesis 11:10 and 26:

11:10 These are [the records of] the generations of Shem. Shem was one hundred years old, and became the father of Arpachshad two years after the flood; 11 and Shem lived five hundred years after he became the father of Arpachshad, and he had [other] sons and daughters. 12 Arpachshad lived thirty-five years, and became the father of Shelah; 13 and Arpachshad lived four hundred and three years after he became the father of Shelah, and he had [other] sons and daughters. 14 Shelah lived thirty years, and became the father of Eber; 15 and Shelah lived four hundred and three years after he became the father of Eber, and he had [other] sons and daughters. 16 Eber lived thirty-four years, and became the father of Peleg; 17and Eber lived four hundred and thirty years after he became the father of Peleg, and he had [other] sons and daughters. 18 Peleg lived thirty years, and became the father of Reu; 19 and Peleg lived two hundred and nine years after he became the father of Reu, and he had [other] sons and daughters. 20 Reu lived thirty-two years, and became the father of Serug; 21 and Reu lived two hundred and seven years after he became the father of Serug, and he had [other] sons and daughters. 22 Serug lived thirty years, and became the father of Nahor; 23 and Serug lived two hundred years after he became the father of Nahor, and he had [other] sons and daughters. 24 Nahor lived twenty-nine years, and became the father of Terah; 25 and Nahor lived one hundred and nineteen years after he became the father of Terah, and he had [other] sons and daughters. 26 Terah lived seventy years, and became the father of Abram, Nahor and Haran.

Circle the name *SHEM* (which means "name" – the term is the basis for the term "Semitic" people). Drop down to the name *Eber* in verse 16 (which means "the region beyond" or the "border rim" and is related to one of the words for WRATH in the Hebrew – the idea of the consistent show of God's principles!). Follow the line of names to *Terah* (the father of Abraham) and you will find at the end of the line the name that means "lifted, raised or exalted father" – Abraham.

God wanted to tell his story, and to do it God told us of a whole line of people that God stewarded along in the process. Some of them were villains, and some were heroes. Many we simply know nothing about. That is true of all of us. We come from a long line of people that God stewarded. Many of them never recognized His hand in their lives, but He was working – in part to get you here at the right time, and the right place.

The truth is that God was at work in our lives even before we knew He was:

Ephesians 1: 4b ...In love 5 He predestined us to adoption as sons through Jesus Christ to Himself, according to the kind intention of His will, 6 to the praise of the glory of His grace, which He freely bestowed on us in the Beloved. 7 In Him we have redemption through His blood, the forgiveness of our trespasses, according to the riches of His grace 8 which He lavished on us. In all wisdom and insight 9 He made known to us the mystery of His will, according to His kind intention which He purposed in Him ... In Him 11 also we have obtained an inheritance, having been predestined according to His purpose

Who works all things after the counsel of His will, 12 to the end that we who were the first to hope in Christ would be to the praise of His glory. 13 In Him, you also, after listening to the message of truth, the gospel of your salvation—having also believed, you were sealed in Him with the Holy Spirit of promise.

Feature Three: You were living your life like others around you, until God's spoke into your life (Gen. 11:27-32).

It is important to note that **Abraham's story doesn't start in a startling way**. Look at the verses at the end of chapter 11. They tell the story of a family man…

- **His father and brothers were a real part of his life:**

11:27   Now these are the records of the generations of Terah. Terah became the father of Abram, Nahor and Haran.

- **His family faced tragedy and pain:**

11:27… and Haran became the father of Lot. 28 Haran died in the presence of his father Terah in the land of his birth, in Ur of the Chaldeans.

- **He had moments of great joy in the album of his life:**

11:29 Abram and Nahor took wives for themselves. The name of Abram's wife was Sarai; and the name of Nahor's wife was Milcah, the daughter of Haran, the father of Milcah and Iscah.

- **He struggled with personal reversals:**

11:30   Sarai was barren; she had no child.

- **His father had dreams that he wasn't able to complete:**

11:31   Terah took Abram his son, and Lot the son of Haran, his grandson, and Sarai his daughter-in-law, his son Abram's wife; and they went out together from Ur of the Chaldeans in order to enter the land of Canaan; and they went as far as Haran, and settled there. 32 The days of Terah were two hundred and five years; and Terah died in Haran.

Now stop and think about what we just saw. **That could have been ANYBODY**. That's the point! God chose to use Abraham – and God chose to speak to you. Until He speaks, it is all the same old stuff. Sunrise, sunset – sunrise, sunset. **Don't miss it. God only works with ordinary people.** We aren't extraordinary until the change God makes. We are water before – and the best wine after. It is the touch of the Master that makes all things new!

Feature Four: God opened your eyes to the "trust exchange" that changed everything. "Get out of thy country." God's promises always come at the same price – Trade what you see for what you cannot, based solely on my Word! (12:1).

Genesis 12:1: Now the LORD said to Abram, "Go forth from your country, and from your relatives and from your father's house, to the land which I will show you."

The line between SAVED and LOST is found in this verse. God spoke and told Abram to change what he was doing. He told Him to GIVE UP what he knew, cherished and trusted in – and lay it demonstrably on the altar so that God could give him the life that God planned for him. The issue of surrender begins – always – with God's word. God spoke. God commanded. God made the conditions.

There are no BIG MEN in Heaven – only small ones - men who know how to fall to their knees and follow instructions. Men who cling deeply to the promises of God because He TOLD THEM TO. Men who know that God delivers on every promise, dries every eye and heals every broken heart.

If you miss the TRUST EXCHANGE, you miss the big picture of surrender... and that is the essential truth that saves us. God's terms are that we surrender our lives to Him, because He is God and we are not. In that moment, He takes up residence in the inviting heart. He works in new ways to make alive dead pathways and synapses.

Feature Five: You saw your life as a reflection of what God can do, not what YOU can do. God promised - "I will": You truly began to see **the source of the blessings** in your life.

Pride isn't indicative of Godliness. (12:2).

Genesis 12:2: And I will make you a great nation, and I will bless you, and make your name great; and so you shall be a blessing.

His emphasis of verse two is not what Abram could do for God, but what God said He would do in and through Abram. No believer struts his stuff. Real believers cling to the cross and the crucified Savior and cry. They know their heart. They know their failings. They know the shame and pain they inflicted on their Savior.

The reminders of the death are a part of our faith. We recall the bread and cup, and say that Jesus paid for our sin with His own broken body and spilled blood. We lower ourselves into a baptismal pool in recognition to all the Godhead – Father, Son and Spirit – and we imitate going into the ground in death and burial. We mark out places of worship with the symbol of a suffering Savior. Jesus and His work is the center of EVERYTHING in my new life!

- Socrates taught for 40 years, Plato for 50, Aristotle for 40, and Jesus for only 3. Yet the influence of Christ's 3-year ministry infinitely transcends the impact left by the combined 130 years of teaching from these men who were among the greatest philosophers of all antiquity.

- Jesus painted no pictures; yet, some of the finest paintings of Raphael, Michelangelo, and Leonardo da Vinci received their inspiration from Him.

- Jesus wrote no poetry; but Dante, Milton , and scores of the world's greatest poets were inspired by Him.

- Jesus composed no music; still Haydn, Handel, Beethoven, Bach, and Mendelssohn reached their highest perfection in the hymns and symphonies they composed in His praise.

- Jesus was most remembered in art, history and music for the moment of His most intense suffering. What the world counted as loss was the moment of His greatest triumph. (liberally adapted, original author unknown).

His pain embodied His power. His blood made no stain, but rather removed the ones that I made with my sin-sick life. The Cross has been the marker for all who know God in this room!

Pittsburgh's airport is one of the biggest and best-equipped in the nation. Two seconds in flying time from the airport and in direct line with one of its busiest runways is the steeple of Union Church. "Ever since the terminal opened," said the pastor, "planes have buzzed the belfry like bees after honey. It got so bad that low-flying jets turned our Sunday evening services into sudden prayer meetings." Reluctant to have their steeple carried away by some careless and unwary pilot, the church topped it with an eight-foot neon-lighted cross. The church is on the highest point near the airport and the lighted cross can be seen at night by planes all the way from the Ohio border. One of the pilots made this interesting comment regarding the lighted cross: "Most of us are using it as a guide to the field." (Pastor Steve Shepherd, *Sermon Central Illustrations*)

Feature Six: You saw the life impact you have on others. Your life stopped being your own. You became a conscious tool in the hand of God to bless other people. "Bless them that bless thee." Acknowledge the nature of His plan. God uses us to reach into the lives of others – our failures have broader consequences! (12:3).

Abram was told that He would be the instrument of blessing to a world God wanted to reach.

Genesis 12:3 And I will bless those who bless you, and the one who curses you I will curse. And in you all the families of the Earth will be blessed.

Jesus told His followers the same thing: John 15: 16 *You did not choose Me but I chose you, and appointed you that you would go and bear fruit, and that your fruit would remain, so that whatever you ask of the Father in My name He may give to you.*

It is obvious to anyone who knows God today that God is working through those who follow Him to bless those around them – even those who do not know Him. That is why believers who can live with an unsaved spouse should stay there – to bring blessing, and hopefully even the message of salvation, into their lives...

1 Corinthians 7:13 And a woman who has an unbelieving husband, and he consents to live with her, she must not send her husband away. 14 For the unbelieving husband is sanctified through his wife, and the unbelieving wife is sanctified through her believing husband; for otherwise your children are unclean, but now they are holy.

Don't forget! Because our witness can have an impact – so can a BAD WITNESS. Our failures as believers will play out in the lives of those around us as well!

Feature Seven: You followed because you understood there was no other way to truly become what you were meant to be. Obedience was the best water mark of identity: "As the Lord spoke." Wear the mark of obedience. It is not brains, nor trust, that is the mark of blessing – it is obedience! (12:4-5).

Genesis 12:4 So Abram went forth as the LORD had spoken to him; and Lot went with him. Now Abram was seventy-five years old when he departed from Haran. 5 Abram took Sarai his wife and Lot his nephew, and all their possessions which they had accumulated, and the persons which they had acquired in Haran, and they set out for the land of Canaan; thus they came to the land of Canaan.

How do you really know if a person is a believer in the Lord?   It isn't by how much they are at church – that might mean they are a professional janitor.   It isn't by how big their *Bible* is – that might mean they cannot see well. It isn't by how long they have been coming to church – that might mean they took longer than others to find a date! You can tell by their **OBEDIENCE** to the principles of the written Word, and their **PASSION** for the Risen Lord!

Feature Eight: Your life is reflected in worship. Gratitude fills your heart for the Lord's kind attention. It isn't about entitlement – what you deserve is the last thing you want to think about!

"Lord appeared – built an altar." Recognize the One Who gives victory and blessing (12:6-8). Note that God was blessed when Abraham gave Him worship in the form of giving back to God his own things!

According to the *Dyersburg State Gazette*, on December 3, 2007 in Dyersburg, TN, 92-year-old Pauline Jacobi had just placed groceries into the driver's side back seat of her tan-colored Toyota Corolla, which was parked in one of the disabled spots near the grocery side entrance of the Wal-Mart Super Center.

"It was later than I usually like to get out," she said. "I'd had a pretty busy day and I was kind of skittish. It was getting dark. But I'd finished my shopping and got into the car. There were people walking to and from, passing back and forth in front of me, so I didn't start my engine so I wouldn't scare them.

"After a few minutes waiting for the right time to move, the front passenger door opened and a tall man, raggedy looking, sat in right next to me. He was bundled up with a heavy jacket and cap," Jacobi said.

"He said 'Give me your money.' I said, 'No, you're not getting my money.' I didn't have anything more than a $10 bill, I think, but I didn't want him to get my medications.

"Then the good Lord took over," Jacobi said. "I said, 'If you kill me, I'm going straight to Heaven. If you kill me, they will find you and kill you – but without Jesus you're going to Hell. You look like you've had an awful time in this world, and as bad as that is, it's nothing compared to Hell. Hell is much worse than anything here ..."Jesus is sitting in the car with me," she told him, as he glanced in the back seat.

"He'll *protect* me if you kill me. I'll go to Heaven, and they'll find you.' I asked him his name," she said. "He said it was Ricky, and he was from Halls."

"Ricky, you drink, don't you?" asked Jacobi. He said he was hungry. I said, 'If you didn't spend your money on drink you'd have money for a meal.' Then I asked him, 'Ricky, would you like to go to Heaven?' 'Yes, I sure would,' he said. 'But I'm afraid the Lord won't take me.'"

"Yes He will. He will take you if you surrender to Him and believe. You have to trust Him and accept Him as your Savior.' "I reached into my purse and opened the clutch bag and pulled out what I think was the $10 bill.

"I said, 'Ricky, I'm going to give you money. Don't spend it on liquor. Get something to eat. I want you to have it. You were going to take it from me, but I'll give it to you.'

"He started to cry. Then he leaned over and gave me a kiss on the cheek.

The shaken man then opened the door and walked into the night. The police report notes from video surveillance of the parking lot that the man was in Jacobi's car for almost 12 minutes before he exited. The recording also shows several dozen shoppers walked by the car during the time Jacobi was ministering to the man. A member of the First Baptist Church for more than 70 years, Jacobi said she frequently prays asking for ways to [lead] people to the Lord.

"I do think maybe this was it," she said. (YouTube.com and Dyersburg State Gazette, Dyersburg TN).

Pauline knows how to look at life. She sees the tapestry from God's side. God's story will become clearer in your life if you look at things from His side of the tapestry.

Reading the Map: Lessons in Genesis

Reading the Map:
Lessons in Genesis

Lesson Eleven: Genesis 12:9-13:4
"How to Kill the Spread of Blessing"

I have had the opportunity to travel in central Italy to several agricultural operations. One of the most delightful opportunities I have ever witnessed can be discovered in a cheese factory. Several basic dairy products are placed in vats with few ingredients, and processed carefully into a variety of cheese products. Cheese is an amazing product. Most all of the ingredients are natural and readily available to the producers. The combination of some of the ingredients seems highly unlikely. Yet there is a process. Add specific ingredients, provide a specific environment, wait a specific amount of time, and cheese will be the result.

There is something comforting in a process that is entirely predictable.

As it is with cheese, so it is with **blessing**. God has a specific process whereby he blesses us and we become a blessing to others. Yet with God's process, **the enemy has also mimicked a process**. His is to draw us away into defeat. His is to aid us in defeat and lost blessing. **The only comfort I can take in this, is that the process is predictable.**

In 2 Corinthians 2:11, Paul tells us that *he* **was not ignorant** of the enemy's devices. In my pastoral experience, I have found many believers that are quite ignorant of the work of the enemy in aiding to their defeat and robbing their blessing. With that in mind, **let's look at the process of slipping from blessing, and the way back to God after we have slipped**.

There are five steps in the enemy's program to push us from the **precipice of blessing** into the **abyss of failure**.

Before we look at the text, let's recall where we are in Abraham's story. It was clear to us in our last study that God's desire was that Abraham, as a believer in a lost world, would **spread blessing to lost men** (cp. **12:3**). Yet, the story we read beginning in Genesis

12:9 shows that his sojourn into Egypt was **NOT** a blessing to the lost – it was a **curse**.

How did Abraham kill the spread of God's blessing? Just as important, what could he do about a lost testimony?

Key Principle: There is a pattern to falling from the place of blessing and making God's goodness turned sour. There is also a process for return.

Sliding Downward into Failure in Five Easy Steps!

Step One: Discontentment.

Genesis 12:9 Abram journeyed on, continuing toward the Negev. 10 Now there was a famine in the land; so Abram went down to Egypt to sojourn there, for the famine was severe in the land.

The discontentment with the "place" God put Abram sent him packing to a "better" place. It also led him into the heart of a series of perils (12:9-10). **Principle: Where God places us is the best place to be.**

I am not suggesting we never move – I am suggesting we never move out of the place where God told us we should be – and that is the difference. When we kick against God's revealed will, we may feel we are getting more of our own way, but we are heading for long-term disaster.

Discontent truly is the first step toward change. The problem is that **not all change is good**. I may become stirred because God wants to do something new in me. Yet, more often than not, I become stirred because of other passions that exist within me. Some of those passions are subject to the enemy, and to the flesh.

"Content makes poor men rich; discontent makes rich men poor." (Benjamin Franklin.)

"In the fifth century, a man named Arenius determined to live a holy life. So he abandoned the conforms of Egyptian society to follow an austere lifestyle in the desert. Yet whenever he visited the great city of Alexandria, he spent time wandering through its bazaars. Asked why, he explained that his heart rejoiced at the sight of all the things he didn't need. Those of us who live in a society flooded with goods and gadgets need to ponder the example of that desert dweller. A typical supermarket in the United States in 1976 stocked 9,000 articles; today it carries 30,000. How many of them are absolutely essential? How many superfluous?" (*Our Daily Bread*, May 26,1994.)

"Years ago, Russell Conwell told of an ancient Persian, Ali Hafed, who "owned a very large farm that had orchards, grain fields, and gardens... and was a wealthy contented man." One day a wise man from the East told the farmer all about diamonds and how wealthy he would be if he owned a diamond mine. Ali Hafed went to bed that night a poor man--poor because he was discontented. Craving a mine of diamonds, he sold his farm to search for the rare stones. He traveled the world over, finally becoming so poor, broken, and defeated that he committed suicide.

One day the man who purchased Ali Hafed's farm led his camel into the garden to drink. As his camel put its nose into the brook, the man saw a flash of light from the sands of the stream. He pulled out a stone that reflected all the hues of the rainbow. The man had discovered the diamond mine of Golcanda, the most magnificent mine in all history. Had Ali Hafed remained at home and dug in his own garden, then instead of death in a strange land, he would have had acres of diamonds." (G. Sweeting, in *Moody Monthly*, May, 1988, p. 95)

I think this significant lesson is that we must learn to be content with what we have, but we are never to be content with what we are. When we are growing in the Lord, when we are surrendering new ground of our heart to Him -- we are changing in ways that are desirable. We must measure our discontent, and search out its root.

Is God trying to move me to higher obedience? Am I trying to move myself to a place of disobedience?

Step Two: Fear.

Genesis 12:11 It came about when he came near to Egypt, that he said to Sarai his wife, "See now, I know that you are a beautiful woman; 12 and when the Egyptians see you, they will say, 'This is his wife'; and they will kill me, but they will let you live.'"

The problems brought on by Abram's choice to walk away from God's revealed place for him led him into problems. In the midst of the peril, fear set in. He found himself frustrated and vulnerable (12:11-12). **Principle: Without the assurance that we are in the center of God's place for us, we are vulnerable to sweeping fear and frustration!**

Notice that the fear first manifested itself in verse 11 when the couple came near to Egypt. Abraham was not only outside of the place that God told him to be, he was nearing the place of the world culture. He was facing his problem of a famine, but he was doing it with his own solution. There is no mention of Abraham seeking God to go teach it. The place God chose for him was north, not south toward Egypt.

All of us have faced a time in our lives when fear dominated us. Perhaps it was a fear that we would be taken advantage of. Perhaps it was a fear that we would be discovered. Yet we all know what fear is.

"During his years as premier of the Soviet Union, Nikita Khrushchev denounced many of the policies and atrocities of Joseph Stalin. Once, as he censured Stalin in a public meeting, Khrushchev was interrupted by a shout from a heckler in the audience.

"You were one of Stalin's colleagues. Why didn't you stop him?"

"Who said that?" roared Khrushchev.

An agonizing silence followed as nobody in the room dared move a muscle. Then Khrushchev replied quietly, "Now you know why." (*Today in the Word*, July 13, 1993)

"God did not give us the spirit of fear," 2 Timothy 1:17 says. Yet we have all experienced fear. One of the reasons we experience it so deeply is because we allow the discontent of our lives to lead us away from the position of strength God has put us in. If you are afraid today it may be because you left the path that God and you were walking together. You're not sure now.

Fear has the ability to create a paralysis within us.

"Black Bart was a professional thief whose very name struck fear as he terrorized the *Wells Fargo Stage Line*. From San Francisco to New York, his name became synonymous with the danger of the frontier. Between 1875 and 1883 he robbed 29 different stagecoach crews. Amazingly, Bart did it all without firing a shot. Because a hood hid his face, no victim ever saw his face. He never took a hostage and was never trailed by a sheriff. Instead, Black Bart used fear to paralyze his victims. His sinister presence was enough to overwhelm the toughest stagecoach guard." (*Today in the Word*, August 8, 1992)

Consider this story: "Five-year old Johnny was in the kitchen as his mother made supper. She asked him to go into the pantry and get her a can of tomato soup, but he didn't want to go in alone. "It's dark in there and I'm scared." She asked again, and he persisted. Finally she said, "It's OK--Jesus will be in there with you." Johnny walked hesitantly to the door and slowly opened it. He peeked inside, saw it was dark, and started to leave when all at once an idea came, and he said: "Jesus, if you're in there, would you hand me that can of tomato soup?" (Charles Allen, *Victory in the Valleys*)

It is not wrong for you to experience fear; it is wrong for you to surrender to it and allow it to dominate your thinking and paralyze your walk. When the storms rage, we call upon the Lord to calm the storm. He may choose to do so. Or he may choose to calm his child in the midst of the storm.

One thing is certain: you will never be the stable, calm and assured believer you are called to be when you are dislodged by discontent.

Step Three: Deception.

Genesis 12:13 Please say that you are my sister so that it may go well with me because of you, and that I may live on account of you.

The **fear** and **vulnerability** led to Abram trying his best to "**cover himself.**" **He did not turn to God for aid**; he **solved the problems in the realm of the flesh**. In the end, he found it easier to **lie**, and the **poison of deception thwarted his testimony** to both his wife and the world. His misplaced trust is a notable tip-off to the problem (i.e. "of you" in 12:13).

"Bob Harris, weatherman for NY TV station WPIX-TV and the nationally syndicated *Independent Network News*, had to weather a public storm of his own making in 1979. Though he had studied math, physics and geology at three colleges, he left school without a degree but with a strong desire to be a media weatherman. He phoned *WCBS-TV*, introducing himself as a Ph.D. in geophysics from Columbia U. The phony degree got him in the door. After a two-month tryout, he was hired as an off-camera forecaster for *WCBS*. For the next decade his career flourished. He became widely known as "Dr. Bob." He was also hired by the *New York Times* as a consulting meteorologist. The same year both the *Long Island Railroad* and then Baseball Commissioner Bowie Kuhn hired him. Forty years of age and living his childhood dream, he found himself in public disgrace and national humiliation when an anonymous letter prompted *WCBS* management to investigate his academic credentials. Both the station and the *New York Times* fired him. His story got attention across the land. He was on *The Today Show*, *The Tomorrow Show*, and in *People Weekly*, among others. He thought he'd lose his home and never work in the media again. Several days later the *Long Island Railroad* and Bowie Kuhn announced they would not fire him. Then *WNEW-TV* gave him a job. He admits it was a dreadful mistake on his part and doubtless played a role in his divorce. "I took a shortcut that turned out to be the long way around, and one day the bill came due. I will be sorry as long as I am alive." (Nancy Shulins, *Journal News*, Nyack, NY)

Principle: The "father of lies" will do his work in us when we have left our "place" and are walking in a way that opens us to deception.

We will be deceived into believing **WE** can solve our problems, and then DECEIVE others as the lies spread. We cannot be an uncompromising testimony to truths we don't believe enough to consistently live! There are no shortcuts. We are called to be people of truth in a world run by a prince of lies. God's people must speak truth. We face an enemy that knows how to bluff us with lies. Because of that, we must stand confidently before the Lord.

In late September 1864 Confederate General Nathan Bedford Forrest was leading his troops north from Decatur, Alabama, toward Nashville. But to make it to Nashville, Forrest would have to defeat the Union Army at Athens, Alabama. When the Union commander, Colonel Wallace Campbell, refused to surrender, Forrest asked for a personal meeting, and took Campbell on an inspection of his troops. But each time they left a detachment, the Confederate soldiers simply packed up and moved to another position, artillery and all. Forrest and Campbell would then arrive at the new encampment and continue to tally up the impressive number of Confederate soldiers and weaponry. By the time they returned to the fort, Campbell was convinced he couldn't win and surrendered unconditionally! (*Today in the Word*, June 27,1993)

Mature believers expect the enemy to throw curveballs and lies at their life. He will summon old attitudes, raise up old fears, make monsters out of dark shadows -- all to get you to become impatient with God's will and spurn God's direction.

Step Four: Hypocrisy.

Genesis 12:14 It came about when Abram came into Egypt, the Egyptians saw that the woman was very beautiful. 15 Pharaoh's officials saw her and praised her to Pharaoh; and the woman was taken into Pharaoh's house. 16 Therefore he treated Abram well for her sake; and gave him sheep and oxen and donkeys and male and female servants and female donkeys and camels.

The encounter Abram had with the world was met amid deception and a total departure from his walk with God. He killed his testimony by reaching out in deception rather than in a genuine walk of integrity (12:14-16).

Principle: We cannot give out what we don't possess. We cannot urge others to trust a God we do not!

Hypocrites have always been around the church.

He made free use of Christian vocabulary. He talked about the blessing of the Almighty and the Christian confessions which would become the pillars of the new government. He assumed the earnestness of a man weighed down by historic responsibility. He handed out pious stories to the press, especially to the church papers. He showed his tattered Bible and declared that he drew the strength for his great work from it as scores of pious people welcomed him as a man sent from God. Indeed, Adolf Hitler was a master of outward religiosity--with no inward reality! (*Today in the Word*, June 3, 1989)

It is the responsibility of every Christian to stand in integrity. When we fail to walk honestly before man and God, we join the side of God's enemy. We inadvertently become part of the problem and not the answer.

We begin to sound like the hypocritical congressman who said when addressing the House of Representatives: Never before have I heard such ill-informed, wimpy, backstabbing drivel as that just uttered by my respected colleague, the distinguished gentleman from Ohio. (E.E. Smith, Wall Street Journal)

A sour heart can be heard in slanted speech. A straying believer cannot hide for very long before the distance between them and God becomes apparent to all who know them well. God's purpose in our life is to be a testimony for him -- but we will fail in this when our mouth is slanted away from truth.

Psalm 15 urges the man of God to stand before man and speak with integrity. It is a prerequisite to walking with God; it is a precursor to being close to Him.

The Step Five: Rotten Fruit.

Genesis 12:17 But the LORD struck Pharaoh and his house with great plagues because of Sarai, Abram's wife. 18 Then Pharaoh called Abram and said, "What is this you have done to me? Why did you not tell me that she was your wife? 19 Why did you say, 'She is my sister,' so that I took her for my wife? Now then, here is your wife, take her and go." 20 Pharaoh commanded his men concerning him; and they escorted him away, with his wife and all that belonged to him.

The encounter with Abram left Pharaoh in worse shape than he was before this "man of God" came to him! In the end, instead of bringing the blessing that should come when a believer enters the scene, Abram brought pain! Pharaoh loathed the God of Abraham (12:17-20)!

Principle: A believer walking in defiance will bring pain and heartache to the people he should bring blessing to!

The shop where you work, the home where you live, the community that you call your own, may actually be suffering by the gap in your life between a true walk with God and a hypocritical "spiritual self-life" that mimics Christianity.

Chuck Swindoll tells the story of a man who bore two faces: Several years ago, in Long Beach, California, a fellow went into a fried chicken place and bought a couple of chicken dinners for himself and his date late one afternoon. The young woman at the counter inadvertently gave him the proceeds from the day-a whole bag of money (much of it cash) instead of fried chicken. After driving to their picnic site, the two of them sat down to open the meal and enjoy some chicken together. They discovered a whole lot more than chicken – over $800!

But he was unusual. He quickly put the money back in the bag. They got back into the car and drove all the way back. Mr. Clean got out, walked in, and became an instant hero. By then the manager was frantic.

The guy with the bag of money looked the manager in the eye and said, "I want you to know I came by to get a couple of chicken dinners and wound up with all this money. Here."

Well, the manager was thrilled to death. He said, "Oh, great, let me call the newspaper. I'm gonna have your picture put in the local newspaper. You're the most honest man I've heard of" to which the guy quickly responded, "Oh no, no don't do that!"

Then he leaned closer and whispered, "You see, the woman I'm with is not my wife...she's, uh, somebody else's wife." (Charles Swindoll, *Growing Deep in the Christian Life,* p. 159-60)

Funny how we uphold one standard in one area of our life, only to utterly violate the truth of a healthy inner life in some other way!

What could Abraham do when he destroyed his testimony?

Abraham left the scene (13:1-4) and returned back to the place God put him. When he came back to his "place" he turned his heart back to God and bowed before Him!

Genesis 13:1 So Abram went up from Egypt to the Negev, he and his wife and all that belonged to him, and Lot with him. 2 Now Abram was very rich in livestock, in silver and in gold. 3 He went on his journeys from the Negev as far as Bethel, to the place where his tent had been at the beginning, between Bethel and Ai, 4 to the place of the altar which he had made there formerly; and there Abram called on the name of the LORD.

I mention this because **there is a pattern to falling from the place of blessing and making God's goodness turn sour. There is also a process for return.** When we discover that we are living a lie we must turn back to where we left the path of our walk with God. We must come back and call on His name. We must celebrate the blessings He has continued to pour on our lives. We cannot turn back and change the past, but we can look upward and change the future.

We can humbly grabbed the edge of His garment, and tearfully seek restoration. Is that your need today? Remember, the same arms that were stretched out at Calvary are still stretched out reaching for you.

Reading the Map:
Lessons in Genesis

Lesson Twelve: Genesis 13:2-18
"Five Secrets of Spreading Blessing"

He had the "Midas touch." His work grew and prospered. His reputation flourished. In every direction he could see a brighter horizon. Life couldn't get better. It wasn't that he never experienced problems, but his life was... well... blessed.

Why does it seem that God pours out on some lives a special set of good things? It is because God puts into play blessings that we can use to bless others... **We are blessed to be a blessing**. To whom much is given - much is required; the standard is raised. Do you know the secrets of spreading blessing?

Key Principle: When my heart is truly generous toward others, there will be those who cannot understand what I am doing!

Abraham learned to receive God's blessings, and he learned how to "turn off the valve" of the blessings. Had he learned the secrets to blessing others?

Secret #1: Know the Source of Generosity (13:2-4).

Genesis 13:2 Now Abram was very rich in livestock, in silver and in gold. 3 He went on his journeys from the Negev as far as Bethel, to the place where his tent had been at the beginning, between Bethel and Ai, 4 to the place of the altar which he had made there formerly; and there Abram called on the name of the LORD.

Abraham's generous heart was rooted in the knowledge of his **undeserved** blessing from God. Coming from a defeat in his life, God cleansed his heart, and God's grace marked Abraham's relationships.

Principle: A right relationship with God nurtures a generous heart, and curbs a critical and judgmental heart.

Abraham had physical blessings. If you ate this morning, so do you and I. If you have clothing in your closet, you have blessing. Yet, at the heart of the blessing is a sense of thankfulness that God has been good.

Abraham had defeats and failures in his life, but they became *Tessa Rae* in the mosaic of his life that taught him about God. On the back of his biggest known failure to date, in the face of the public exposure of his unfaithfulness to the standard of truth and of his God – on the revelation that he was willing to trade his wife's purity for his own safety – he was able to receive such cleansing to come back to blessing by coming back to worship. He fell before God a broken and sinful man.

Look at the process closely in the verses:

1. Abraham took his fortune back to the Negev – that is the place HE CHOSE to go afterGod gave him the land to the north (13:2). **Surrender to God preceded generosity that was fruitful. Give your heart to God before you give your stuff to others** – or it will have no real meaning!

2. Abraham did not remain in the Negev, though the atmosphere and appearance was what more familiar to him. He continued to press on, taking his family north to the mountains of Judah, stopping only when he came to the place where God spoke to him (13:3).

Submission to God of personal comfort preceded generosity that was fruitful. Give up on having everything you want before you give away your things to others, and you will be joyful in the giving!

3. He went back to the marker of his life where he responded to God's promises to him (13:4), to the place of the altar of sacrifice. **Sacrifice for God preceded generosity that bore fruit in the lives of his companions.** People who have celebrated joyfully with God at the altar can give with a different heart. They know this life is not all there is, and that people are not all who SEE what is given – and how.

All of us have to face the reality that we are selfish. People in ministry are no different.

Have you heard that story of the believer who left this life and arrived in Heaven? He was being given a tour of Heaven and he saw a friend of his drive by in a beautiful Mercedes.

He said, "Boy, this is great!"

"Oh, yes," St. Peter said, "your friend was really generous on Earth, we had a lot to work with. Your transportation up here depends on your generosity down there."

Then Peter gave him his transportation: a Honda motor scooter. He said, "Wait a minute, he gets a Mercedes, I get a scooter?"

"That's right; it's all we had to work with."

The guy drove off in a huff. A week later Peter saw this guy all smiles and said, "You feeling better now?"

The guy said, "Yea, I have ever since I saw my preacher go by on a skate board!"

Nearly a century ago, a famous English preacher described in vivid detail the practice of one particular lord of the manor. Every year on Christmas day, this lord gave all the poor people who were his subjects a generous basket of food. Every person brought a basket with him and the lord's custom was to fill the basket completely. Each time they came, year after year, the baskets got bigger and bigger, until the lord wondered how they could stagger away under the weight of all that food on the way home. But no matter how large the basket was, he filled it every time.

They came because they knew about his wealth and because they trusted in his free-flowing generosity. He said he did this because he knew what it was like to be hungry, and because the bounty of the land was given at the good hand of God!

Late in the New Testament is a small "post card" sized letter of John the Apostle that we call 3 John. The old apostle wrote to a church leader named Gaius, and said these words: 3 John 1:1 The elder to the beloved Gaius, whom I love in truth. 2 Beloved, I pray that in all respects you may prosper and be in good health, just as your soul prospers.

The physical prosperity the apostle John wished for Gaius was held in relationship with Gaius' pre-existent spiritual prosperity. John writes: "even as thy soul prospers."

Principle: To wish physical prosperity on someone without their first attaining spiritual maturity is dangerous. Why?

Because...

- If the soul is not first prospering in humility, wealth will make it proud.
- If the soul is not first prospering in gentleness, wealth will make it rough.
- If the soul is not first prospering in generosity, wealth will make it stingy.
- If the soul is not first prospering in faith, wealth will make it doubt.
- If the soul it not first prospering in selflessness, wealth will make it selfish.

"The prosperity of fools shall destroy them." Prov. 1:32

Secret #2: Understand the Problem (13:5-7).

Genesis 13:5 Now Lot, who went with Abram, also had flocks and herds and tents. 6 And the land could not sustain them while dwelling together, for their possessions were so great that they were not able to remain together. 7 And there was strife between the herdsmen of Abram's livestock and the herdsmen of Lot's livestock. Now the Canaanite and the Perizzite were dwelling then in the land.

Generosity and other person-centered living is **not** the norm in our world. People are self-interested, which causes constant strife (James 4:1).

We have learned to LOCK EVRYTHING. You would think that the problem of stealing would be reduced as more people have access to greater wealth. That is not true. In fact, **it is not the lack of physical wealth that leads people to steal, it is a poverty of soul** – a disconnection from God and His moral character – that leads people to steal and justify the act in their value system. When you live surrounded by corrupt morality, it is hard to recall that God did not design life to be what we have made it become.

Principle: When my heart is truly generous toward others, there will be those who cannot understand what I am doing!

One preacher I heard recently shared: "A pastor had a farmer friend in his congregation and they were talking over the fence one day. The pastor asked the farmer, "Abe, if you had one hundred horses, would you give me fifty?"

Abe said, "Certainly." The pastor asked, "If you had one hundred cows, would you give me fifty?" Abe said, "Yes."

Then the pastor asked, "If you had two pigs, would you give me one?" Abe said, "Now cut that out, Pastor; you know I have two pigs!" (origin unknown).

Generosity sounds good in the abstract; many Christians picture themselves giving away half their lottery winnings. Fewer, it seems, can part with one pig.

Look more closely into verses five to seven:

1. **Lot and Abraham BOTH had physical prosperity**. Staying close to those who know God is always a good idea. **When the blessings are poured out on God's people, be one of them – or at least stay close. It is best to bring an umbrella. In the absence of that, bring a friend who owns one!** (13:5)

2. **Lot and Abraham's things were causing each of them problems** – because the territory was too small for so many flocks and herds. Even good things raise issues and need to be

carefully managed. Even physical prosperity causes difficulties – and that is why the heart needs to be in order first (13:6).

3. **There was strife between the herdsmen**. The people who didn't own the flocks were more intense about the conflict than those who did. They saw the **interests** of their master – but they didn't mimic the **heart** of the master! The same can be said of believers today. Often we get so interested in protecting the reputation and territory of the Master we forget to have the heart of the Master in doing so! (13:7)

Secret #3: See Problems as Opportunities to be Generous (13:8-9).

Genesis 13:8 So Abram said to Lot, "Please let there be no strife between you and me, nor between my herdsmen and your herdsmen, for we are brothers. 9 Is not the whole land before you? Please separate from me; if to the left, then I will go to the right; or if to the right, then I will go to the left."

Generosity is "acts that are based on a deliberate intention to help another gain what they need to become what God intends them to be (to reach their potential for God)." When Abraham saw the tensions, he used the opportunity to better Lot's fortunes!

Principle: Opportunities are either viewed as obstacles (and chafed at) or as opportunities (and carefully responded to).

Consider this tale: "In 2005 Thomas Cannon died. He was 79. When he was three years old his father died, his mother remarried and raised their family in a three-room shack without running water or electricity. As an adult, Thomas went to work for the postal service. He never made more than $25,000 a year. Upon retirement, he and his wife lived in poverty. Yet, over the course of his life, he gave away more than $156,000. His gifts were mainly in the form of checks in the amount of $1,000 to people he read about in the newspaper who were going through hard times. His biographer commented, "Not many people would consider living in a house in a poor neighborhood without central heat, air conditioning, or a telephone, and working overtime so they could save money to give away." (*Thomas Cannon had*

Little Money to Give, Omaha Sunday World Herald, July 2005, p. 13A; Margaret Edds, "Cannon's Canon," Hampton Roads.com, 7/24/05. From a sermon by Monty Newton, "Asking for Money: Biblical Principles for Generosity" 6/28/2009)

Look at verses 8-9 more closely:

Abraham didn't deny the problem, but acted to bring things back to the right place. Problems, like stinky fish, have a way of letting you know they haven't gone away. Ignore them and they will grow stronger until you cannot avoid their stench. (13:8)

The heart of Abraham's request was not to get his flocks an advantage – it was to get the relationship restored for everyone. **Truly generous people are about PEOPLE not simply PEACE and QUIET.** (13:9)

Abraham faced that they could not remain together in space, but he devised a way for them to remain together in their hearts – for him to show preference for Lot's family. Preferring another above ourselves opens the heart of the recipient. Hold that door for another. Stop and acknowledge the people you meet and show them that they are not a bother. (13:9)

Secret #4: Delight in the Progress of the Other (13:10-11).

Genesis 13:10 Lot lifted up his eyes and saw all the valley of the Jordan, that it was well watered everywhere—this was before the LORD destroyed Sodom and Gomorrah—like the garden of the LORD, like the land of Egypt as you go to Zoar. 11 So Lot chose for himself all the valley of the Jordan, and Lot journeyed eastward. Thus they separated from each other.

Abraham was energized by the progress of his nephew, Lot. He was not resistant, but reinforcing and encouraging.

Principle: Nothing kills a generous heart more than the venom of jealousy.

Years ago on Candid Camera, children were used in an experiment about generosity. The children were placed by themselves in a room with a plate of cookies. On the plate were at least two cookies; there may have been more, but one of the cookies was very large. The adult left the room and the kids were allowed to take a cookie. You know, they all took the big one. One boy was challenged as to why he took the biggest cookie. Alan Funt, the host, told the boy, "All you left me to eat was the little cookie. I would have eaten the little cookie and given you the biggest one." Without a blink the boy responded, "Then you got the one you wanted." (A-Z Sermon Illustrations).

Generosity is a tough thing to learn. We should put others first.

Look again at verses 10-11:

1. Lot chose what seemed best for him based on a view of prosperity, not based on the **character** of the people who lived in that place (13:10). **Remember: long after the prosperity fades, the character of your friends makes a deep mark on your life!**

2. Lot chose a flat place because it looked more settled, but it was a much more turbulent place (13:11). The Jordan Valley is part of the world's largest rift, and subject to mighty quakes and seismic events – as he would eventually discover. **What looks easier is often built on a shallow foundation in a dangerous place!**

Secret #5: See God's Promises to YOU as the continued source of Happiness and Security (13:12-18).

Return to Genesis and keep reading for a moment... *Genesis 13:12 Abram settled in the land of Canaan, while Lot settled in the cities of the valley, and moved his tents as far as Sodom. 13 Now the men of Sodom were wicked exceedingly and sinners against the LORD. 14 The LORD said to Abram, after Lot had separated from him, "Now lift up your eyes and look from the place where you are, northward and southward and eastward and westward; 15 for all the land which you see, I will give it to you and to your descendants forever. 16 I will make your descendants as the dust of the earth, so that if anyone can number the dust of the earth, then your descendants can also be numbered. 17 Arise, walk about the land through its length and breadth; for I will give it to you." 18 Then Abram moved his tent and came and dwelt by the oaks of Mamre, which are in Hebron, and there he built an altar to the LORD.*

Abraham got a divine endorsement of blessing in light of his generous heart. You cannot out give God, and He will care for those whose heart is truly generous toward others.

Principle: We are never so tall as when we stoop to help others!

Look very closely at the closing verses of this section.

- 13:12 says "Abraham **settled**" and "Lot **settled.**"
- 13:12 also says "Lot **moved** his tents as far as Sodom" and 13:13:18 says "Abraham moved his tent and came and dwelt by the oaks of Mamre."

What moved Lot was the city filled with men that were not following God (13:12-13).

What moved Abraham were the promises of God for his children and future (13:14) and a place to build an altar of worship (13:18).

Abraham lived life for God and for those God put in his life – and it was rewarded back to him!

Principle: Generosity is the platform for testimony!

Lee, a reporter for *the Chicago Tribune* and a self-professed atheist, was sitting at his desk on Christmas Eve. A slow news day he found himself reminiscing about the Delgado family that he had featured while writing a series of articles about Chicago's neediest people a few days earlier.

The Delgado's were comprised of a grandmother named Perfecta and her two granddaughters, Jenny age 13 and her sister Lydia 11 years old. He remembered how unprepared he was when he walked into their two room apartment on the west side of Chicago for the interview; bare halls and bare walls, no furniture, no rugs, nothing but a kitchen table and a handful of rice in the cupboards. He learned during the interview that Jenny and Lydia only had one short-sleeved dress apiece, plus a thin gray sweater that they shared. On cold days when the girls walked the half-mile to school, one of the girls would start with the sweater and then give it to the other at the halfway mark. It was all they had. Perfecta wanted more for her granddaughters and would gladly have worked, but her severe arthritis and age made work too difficult and painful.

Since it was a slow news day Lee decided to check out a car and drive to Chicago's west side to check up on the Delgado's. When Jenny opened the door he couldn't believe what he saw!

His article on the Delgado's had touched the hearts of many subscribers who responded with furniture and appliances, rugs, dozens of coats, scarves and gloves. The girls wouldn't have to share a sweater any longer. There were cartons and cartons and boxes of food everywhere. They had so much food that the cupboards and closets couldn't contain it. Someone had even donated a Christmas tree, and under it were mounds of presents and thousands of dollars in cash! Lee was astonished! But what astonished him the most was what he found Perfecta and her granddaughters doing. They were preparing to give most of it away.

"Why would you give so much of this away?" Lee asked.

Perfecta responded, "Our neighbors are still in need. We cannot have plenty while they have nothing. This is what Jesus would want us to do."

Lee was dumbfounded. After regaining his composure he asked Perfecta another question. He wanted to know what she and the girls thought about the generosity that was shown to them.

Again, Lee was not prepared for the answer. She said, "This is wonderful; this is very good. We did nothing to deserve this; it's all a gift from God. But," she added, "it is not His greatest gift, Lee. No, we celebrate that tomorrow. Jesus."

Lee was speechless as he drove back to the office. In the quiet of his car he noted a couple of observations. He had plenty and along with it plenty of anxiety, while the Delgado's despite their poverty had peace. Lee had everything and yet wanted more, but the Delgado's had nothing and yet knew generosity. Lee had everything and yet his life was as bare as the Delgado's apartment prior to the article running. And yet the Delgado's who had nothing were filled with hope, contentment and had a spiritual certainty. Even though Lee had so much more than the Delgado's, he longed for what they had in their poverty. From a sermon by Bryan Fink *Christmas is for all the Lees/Leighs of the World* (12/25/2008)

Is your heart generous? Great! God can use that!

Reading the Map:
Lessons in Genesis

Lesson Thirteen: Genesis 14:1-24
"Focal Point"

It was an incredibly cold morning, and the two men were sitting in their perch, twenty feet off of the ground, waiting for a buck to walk across the meadow. They had seen him here before, but never had a clear shot. Today, they hoped, would be the day. For two hours they trudged back into the woods the night before, and they sat until the breaking of the sun on that cold winter morning – hoping against hope that all the cold and discomfort would be worth the day's catch. Another hour went by and one of the men decided that he needed to leave the tree for a necessary stop outside. He strapped his rifle over his back and unfurled the canvas quietly, making his way down the makeshift ladder to the ground. He usually checked the safety on the rifle – almost always – but not that day. His fingers were so cold that he found it difficult to grip the spindles of the ladder. His right foot missed its target and his left hand gave way, causing him to fall backwards off the ladder and hit the hard cold ground with great force. The attempt to grab a branch turned into a wayward grab of the rifle's trigger, and a shot rang out just as the man hit the ground. Looking down from above in horror, his partner scurried downward to find his friend bleeding profusely from his leg, with a terrible knot on his head, and – as if that weren't enough one obviously broken arm. Far from the highway, the man took off his belt to stop the bleeding in his friend's leg, hoisted up his body, broken bones and all, and carried him on the long walk to the car...

She wanted to try it just once. She had been to many parties and she was tired of looking like a prude. She never took so much as an aspirin – but she was graduating and everyone thought she was "the church girl," so she agreed to try the drug one time. Amazed, her friends watched as she went from her normal controlled self to a clearly out of control wild woman. There were at least four guys at the party that were all ready to take advantage of the situation, and they did just that. She has never recovered from her loss of virginity and destruction of her reputation – a great public flame out of testimony. When she came into her youth Pastor's office, she was facing an unwanted pregnancy, a destroyed testimony and a crushed self-image. She felt guilty, stupid, used...

Both of these situations were real. I cannot say they ended badly because, in one sense, they never really ended. The hunter got to the hospital, and the young woman is now a single mother, one of the nearly two million out of wedlock births in 2009 in the US.

I mention the two stories to ask this question, "**How do we respond when a brother or sister does something really stupid?**" Do we celebrate their defeat in our hearts because they "got what they deserved" when things went sour?

How do we offer grace when we face the fallen, especially when their choices led them to the fall?

God has a good word on this in a model from the first book of the *Bible*. This was a set of directions that God knew we all would need as he mapped out the beginnings for us in Genesis. We are in the middle of and the story of Abraham, the man who had a life defined by God's blessings, perhaps more than any other we can quickly think of in Scripture.

In Genesis 14, Abraham learned **to spread blessing by spreading God's mercy and grace**. It was every bit as tough for him as it is for us today, but it has always been one of the ways God showed Himself to hurting people.

The Problem - Lot set up his own problems, by choosing what "looked good" (13:10a), but what was obviously run by unwise and **wicked** (13:13) people. In addition to their pagan wickedness, the choices of the leadership of Sodom and Gomorrah showed them to be utterly unwise even in everyday matters (14:1-12):

1) Not realistic: They unwisely chose the PEOPLE to fight.

Genesis 14:1 And it came about in the days of Amraphel king of Shinar, Arioch king of Ellasar, Chedorlaomer king of Elam, and

Tidal king of Goiim, 2 that they made war with Bera king of Sodom, and with Birsha king of Gomorrah, Shinab king of Admah, and Shemeber king of Zeboiim, and the king of Bela (that is, Zoar). 3 All these came as allies to the valley of Siddim (that is, the Salt Sea). 4 Twelve years they had served Chedorlaomer, but the thirteenth year they rebelled.

14:1-4 Setting: The "big guns" in Shinar, Ellasar (Modern Iraq), Elam (Persian Gulf and Western Iran) and the other nations (Goiim) of the east made war against the five cities of the Jordan valley: Sodom, Gomorrah, Admah, Zeboim and Zoar. The small powers chose to rebel and picked the fight.

2) Not Circumspect: They unwisely chose the PLACE to fight.

Genesis 14:5 In the fourteenth year Chedorlaomer and the kings that were with him, came and defeated the Rephaim in Ashteroth-karnaim and the Zuzim in Ham and the Emim in Shaveh-kiriathaim, 6 and the Horites in their Mount Seir, as far as El-paran, which is by the wilderness. 7 Then they turned back and came to En-mishpat (that is, Kadesh), and conquered all the country of the Amalekites, and also the Amorites, who lived in Hazazon-tamar. 8 And the king of Sodom and the king of Gomorrah and the king of Admah and the king of Zeboiim and the king of Bela (that is, Zoar) came out; and they arrayed for battle against them in the valley of Siddim, 9 against Chedorlaomer king of Elam and Tidal king of Goiim and Amraphel king of Shinar and Arioch king of Ellasar—four kings against five.

In 14:5-9, the Gulf powers decided to come and push through Canaan and into northern Africa. They swung around through the wilderness of Sinai and Paran, and into TransJordan, sweeping every kingdom under their feet. The four eastern kings lined up to battle the five plain kings in the Jordan Valley near the Dead Sea – in a valley close to their own city. They saw them coming, and had sufficient opportunities to stop the advance far from their home.

3) Not Prepared: They unwisely chose a PLAN for defense.

Genesis 14:10 Now the valley of Siddim was full of tar pits; and the kings of Sodom and Gomorrah fled, and they fell into them. But those who survived fled to the hill country. 11 Then they took all the goods of Sodom and Gomorrah and all their food supply, and departed. 12 They also took Lot, Abram's nephew, and his possessions and departed, for he was living in Sodom.

14:10-12 The kings of the plain seemed ill prepared for **territory that should have been familiar** and were defeated by obstacles that should have been obvious to them, but it broke their lines and many fled away. The eastern kings stripped Sodom and Gomorrah and took away those who remained at the city – including Lot.

Lot chose to pitch his tent toward Sodom (13:12b) and remained even when it became obvious what kind of men they were (4:12).

Their prosperity made living among them attractive, but would have obvious ramifications for the children of Lot! The end result of the choice was that **Lot's mistakes cost him his freedom and future!**

Before we go further, for the benefit of everyone who is still in the grips of decision making, **we should point out the danger that Lot demonstrates**.

Paul warned the Corinthians (1 Cor. 15) in his discussion to correct those who were saying that the resurrection was not a literal, real event that (15:33) *Do not be deceived: "Bad company corrupts good morals."* 15:34 *Become sober-minded as you ought, and stop sinning; for some have no knowledge of God. I speak this to your shame.*

He couldn't be clearer. There are people we should not allow in our hearts and our lives. These are the people who scoff at God's Word and God's principles. If the young woman I mentioned a few moments ago had distanced herself from the encouragement of so called "friends," her life would be different today. Who you choose to spend your time with, be they in your iPod, or your TV, or in your home or car – who you choose to spend your time with will frame much of how you view the world, and dramatically alter the nature of temptation in your life. That's important, but that isn't our main lesson.

The main character of this chapter is not Lot, it is Abraham. He was an obedient (albeit imperfect) believer that was about to have a Tuesday afternoon turn into an emergency because of the stupid choices of someone he loved. He was about to face the need to spread blessing by offering undeserved favor to a dim wit.

Wrong focus kills grace. Grace emerges only when the focus is correct.

Key Principle: When grace is shared with the undeserving party, God's blessing (intimacy and relationship with Him) is spread.

How can you do that? How can you offer grace when you want to throttle the guy or gal who did the dumb thing that caused the painful problem? You do it by preparation. Prepare your life NOW by changing your focus...

Six Points of Focus that Expose the Grace of God through My Life:

#1: Focus on Needs over Lessons.

Genesis 14:13 Then a fugitive came and told Abram the Hebrew. Now he was living by the oaks of Mamre the Amorite, brother of Eshcol and brother of Aner, and these were allies with Abram. 14 When Abram heard that his relative had been taken captive, he led out his trained men, born in his house, three hundred and eighteen, and <u>went in pursuit</u> as far as Dan.

Abraham went to deal with the problem without wasting time to ascribe blame. Lot's choice led him to step into the conflict of the region, and it cost him his freedom (14:1-12), but Abraham **focused on the rescue first, not the cause of the problem**.

Grace saw the need of another as more important than any lesson they could teach!

Abraham could have, out of embarrassment before his allies, shied away from helping for fear that they would "get the wrong idea" about his commitments. He simply focused on the rescue first.

The heart of the Pharisee is more geared toward making the point than helping the hurt one. It is found in one who focuses on the lesson, but not the person. God is about people first.

When drowning, a man doesn't need pithy sayings on why jumping in the river was a stupid idea. The heart of a rescuer must be prepared to teach through an active love, not a passive denial. There are times when that love will take a hard form (to reject enabling), but we must be careful not to play that option too **quickly** in the hopes of maintaining personal righteousness. If we are to be like Jesus, He made Himself of "no reputation." He did not seek a bad reputation, it simply was not His focus (14:13-14). Love and justice run in opposite directions. If you want one, you do not truly want the other. If God offers me what I deserve, it will be a swift and just lightning bolt followed by a dusty ash pile. I prefer love for me – but what about the other guy?

#2: Focus on Opportunities over Schedules.

Genesis 14:14 When Abram heard that his relative had been taken captive, he led out his trained men, born in his house, three hundred and eighteen, and went in pursuit as far as Dan.

Grace saw the urgency of rescue as more important than any plan he had already! Abraham heard about the troubles and immediately mobilized his assets to help (14:13- 14). The opportunity to be a vessel of grace will come **at the moment that God chooses, exposed by circumstance**.

In order to respond as God would have me, I must be prepared before the circumstance is exposed. The issue is heart preparation. If I am overtired, stirred over some unrelated issue, or just consumed in myself – I will miss the open door when it presents itself.

#3: Focus on Possibilities over Problems.

Genesis 14:15 He divided his forces against them by night, he and his servants, and defeated them, and pursued them as far as Hobah, which is north of Damascus.

Grace requires not only action but some creativity to help where rescue was needed! Abraham began by pulling in those who had been equipped to deal with military issues (note in verse 14 "trained men"). Though walking with God and within His promises, Abraham **made no presumption that planning was unnecessary**. He had the men trained before the problem arose – because he was in touch with the issues of his day.

This is especially an issue in the day when we have become accustomed to the 24/7 access to anything we need. With the advent of cell phones we call constantly, interrupting others because we refuse to plan or prepare. My lack of preparation must not become the emergency that derails those around me – I need to focus on planning.

Problems will arise, and I cannot anticipate that others will rescue me, or I will draw the energy down of those who God has built up to show grace to another. As the believer, I am the vessel of His grace, and should not be the bottomless pit recipient of emergency aid. Rather than picketing about the issues and inequalities, **he spent his time before the crisis preparing**.

Next, he **actively led the men in the rescue**. He did not simply sit back and plan the risk of other people's resources and lives – he expended himself. Grace is best portrayed in the inconvenient gesture. God pronounces Himself eloquently through the mouth of one who bends far without complaint. Only if we allow ourselves to be used by God does He speak through our lives. The primary issue of service is that it is active and often inconvenient. That is what makes it an opportunity for God to speak through our actions!

Next, his ingenuity showed in that he **outsmarted the opposing army** by doing the unexpected (14:15). The notion that Abraham knew he was doing right did not mean that he assumed some divine advantage and became haphazard in his plan. He took on the challenge and applied every resource to the rescue. Because he surrounded himself with trained men, he no doubt sought and followed their advice on how to proceed.

Finally, Abraham pursued the army that held the captives. He didn't simply "get what he needed" and leave. He made sure that every aspect of the intervention was complete in order to affect the best possible outcome. He could not offer at that moment every insight to Lot on how his choices led him into trouble, but rather he could care for any immediate counter-attack, and take full advantage of the immediate victory (14:15).

#4: Focus on Influence over Immediate Response.

Genesis 14:16 He brought back all the goods, and also brought back his relative Lot with his possessions, and also the women, and the people. 17 Then after his return from the defeat of Chedorlaomer and the kings who were with him, the king of Sodom went out to meet him at the valley of Shaveh (that is, the King's Valley).

Grace always focused on expanding the work of God in PEOPLE by reaching into their needs! Bringing back the goods was probably not very difficult in general. There is always enthusiasm for the spoils of victory. Yet, Abraham was careful to bring **everyone** home to their families (14:16-17). This was not simply the marine "Leave no man behind" issue, as it included every person who had their life overturned by troubles in the midst of the struggle. Abraham was under no obligation he made personally to rescue the others, but doing so would offer him a
platform to minister in the lives of the other families. **He wanted the access to that stage, but had to earn the right to speak.**

We live in a time when believers want access to stages they haven't earned, simply because they are certain that they are correct in what they are saying. We may know God and His Word, but our practical help alone offers us an access to the lives of people around us – people don't care what you know until they know that you care about them!

The end of 14:16 clearly shows that Abraham took advantage of the victory to repatriate every person that was dislodged from their life. He had **compassion** on every person wounded by the struggle. He **didn't question the righteousness or role of those he helped** – because his compassionate focus opened them to his God. Nothing in the text suggests that those he saved expressed personal thankfulness, or moved toward his life message of the one true God.

#5: Focus on Offering Praise over Receiving Recognition.

Genesis 14:18 And Melchizedek king of Salem brought out bread and wine; now he was a priest of God Most High. 19 He blessed him and said, ""Blessed be Abram of God Most High, Possessor of Heaven and Earth; 20 and blessed be God Most High, Who has delivered your enemies into your hand." He gave him a tenth of all.

Grace seeks to recognize the blessing and purposes of God when they show themselves! Abraham offered a tithe of all he had in recognition to God's goodness (14:18-20) and the relationship of others to God. As the star of the hour, Abe could have tried to pull more recognition to himself, but instead he deliberately chose to focus the attention on another man's status before God.

#6: Focused on Eternal Clarity over Temporal Benefit.

Genesis 14:21 The king of Sodom said to Abram, "Give the people to me and take the goods for yourself." 22 Abram said to the king of Sodom, "I have sworn to the LORD God Most High, possessor of Heaven and Earth, 23 that I will not take a thread or a sandal thong or anything that is yours, for fear you would say, 'I have made Abram rich.' 24 I will take nothing except what the young men have eaten, and the share of the men who went with me, Aner, Eshcol, and Mamre; let them take their share.

A man of grace was able to be a testimony by giving with no misunderstanding about his open intention to help without strings (14:21-24). Abraham offered everything back to the kings!

Wrong focus kills grace. Grace emerges only when the focus is correct. When grace is shared with the undeserving party, God's blessing (intimacy and relationship with Him) is spread.

Reading the Map:
Lessons in Genesis

Lesson Fourteen: Genesis 15:1-2
"Understanding the Map Key"

"We are hopelessly lost!" she cried as he made the turn onto the dusty, dirt road. "But I followed the map... how could this happen?"

"I don't know and I don't care!" She said angrily. "I knew we were going to be late. We should have 'Googled' the directions! I know how to read a map! I just can't understand what some of these symbols mean!"

This little argument, heard in automobiles all across the US, illustrates the key principle of Genesis 15. We must not only possess the map, but understand how God offers directions – what the symbols on the map mean.

I want to reach into the *Bible* in this lesson and talk about some **specific principles relating to knowing and following the will of God in your life.** This is a subject that can be seen in many places in Scripture, and has been tackled by many great sermons of excellent *Bible* expositors in the past.

I remember when I was in college Dr. John McArthur shared some messages on the will of God, and opened with this thought:

"Some people treat the will of God as if it is a brass ring, or a special token that only some select few get in life. Some people treated it as if God is being very cryptic about His desires for us. It's like they're going to be walking down the street one day and trip and fall, landing with their nose on the map of India -- and then they'll know that's where God wants them to go. Other people wait for the shaking of the bed in the middle of the night when God would say: "Go to New York!" They believe that God will speak to them in the still of the night, and that is the way they should learn to follow Him." (from my notes of his talk to students).

Obviously we do not believe that God's will is something cryptic. In fact, Genesis 15 reminds us that God's will can be known and followed. **The will of God in your life is not an "extra," it is essential, and God knows how to reveal it!**

Key Principle: Following God's will requires thought, reflection and inspection – BUT IT CAN BE KNOWN.

In our text, God met Abraham a fourth time, and **each time God met him, He added to the promises He made on the previous meetings:**

- **Emptying Promise**: The first meeting was in **Genesis 12:1-3**, when God told Abram to move out to a country God would show him, and that **God would make Abram a blessing** to all nations.

- **Defining Promise**: The second meeting was recorded in **12:7** when God told Abram that he would **receive all the land he could see** for his descendants.

- **Extending Promise**: Another meeting was recorded in **13:14**, after Abraham rescued Lot and gave tithes to Melchisedek. God promised Abraham the **land allotment would be forever** his for his family.

- **Specifying Promise**: This fourth meeting between God and Abraham was the record of a vision (**15:1-21**), where God made an additional promise: Your **household** will have great **reward**. Abram asks "How?" God replies, "**Your seed will be many**, and come from YOU!"

Five Principles on finding and following God's will:

Principle #1: Encouragement Principle: God recognizes our need to be encouraged when the rewards are distant, and

offers His Word to lift us! God met Abraham to respond to his fear of constant conflict and limited reward (15:1).

*Genesis 15:1 After these things the word of the LORD came to Abram in a vision, saying, "Do not fear, Abram, I am a shield to you; **Your reward** shall be very great."*

Genesis 15:1 is a simple statement made by God to Abraham. On the surface, God is simply saying to Abraham, "I want to encourage you with a future reward that will be yours." Yet, look closely at three phrases and you will see that God is saying much more. **God's encouragement of his man or woman can include three specific parts:**

Part One: Intimate understanding: When God encourages a man, He does so first by understanding our makeup so thoroughly that He can address our inner fear.

When God spoke a fourth time to Abraham, He had knowledge that Abraham appeared to be dreading his future in the words "do not fear" (tir-a is from yaw-ray': to dread or make afraid). What a strange thing to say to a man who has just fought a hard battle in order to get his nephew Lot saved from the kings that took him captive. God knew that Abraham was courageous when it came to warfare, but fearful when it came to the application of God's promises - specifically about his family's future.

God's will offers encouragement by directing itself to our real inner fear.

Do you recall Moses and his encounter with God as he was leading the people in the wilderness?   In Exodus 33: 12-13 Moses said to God, "Look, you tell me, 'Lead this people,' but you don't let me know whom You're going to send with me. You tell me, **'I know you well and you are special to me.'** If I am so special to You, let me in on Your plans. That way, I will continue being special to You. Don't forget, this is Your people, Your responsibility." 14 God said,   "My presence will go with you.   I'll see the journey to the end."   15-16 Moses said, "If Your presence doesn't take the lead here, call this trip off right now. How else will it be known that You're with me in this, with me and Your people? Are you traveling with us or not? How else will we know that we're special, I and Your people, among all other people on this planet Earth?" *(The Message).*

God's intimate knowledge of us, and all that He calls us to do should encourage us -- God is not leading us into the dark, and He knows us better than we know ourselves. That means He knows what I can bear, and when I will break.

Pastor Eric Fary said it this way: The immensely vast universe of the heavens declares the glory of a God Who is even bigger and greater. The Hubble Space Telescope sends back infrared images of faint galaxies that are billions of light years away. A light year is six trillion miles - per second - that's over 186,000 miles a second, fast enough to go around the Earth between 7 and 8 times every second. If the rays from the sun were traveling at that speed, they would take several minutes just to arrive at Earth -- that's how far the distance is from that star to one of its closer planets. It's hard for our minds to even fathom that sort of thing, but what is truly more amazing is that Isaiah 40:26 says that every single one of the billions and trillions of stars, is known by God individually – He knows them all *by name.* That same God knows and cares about every sparrow that falls to the ground. That same God knows and cares about you – astounding and surprising as that may seem in the bigger scheme of things – He knows you better than you know yourself. He knows the exact number of hairs on your head, Jesus says.

Part Two: Need for shelter: God claimed in the text to be a "shield" (maw-gane') to Abraham. **Abraham needed encouragement that God knew exactly where he was and what he had been doing. He also needed to know that he could rest now in the powerful shield that is our God**. Several commentators make the note that the Hebrew term may be used to denote "sovereign" or the term "shield". Though both were the case, the term shield seems to be more in order, "What is God saying?" On the heels of a hard-fought victory, Abraham needed a place of rest. **God's will offers encouragement by offering us a safe place to hide -- obedience to Him and intimacy with Him; He becomes our refuge.**

Part Three: Hope of reward: Abraham had just finished paying tithes to Melchisedek for protection. He had given back to the King of Sodom all of the spoils of the victory for which he and his men had just fought. He gave them back their women and their slaves. Abraham needed the encouragement of God that his integrity and hard-fought battles were not without compensation (saw-kawr': wages or compensation). God's will offers encouragement by reminding us that there is a reward that comes to those who follow Him.

Principle #2: Inspection Principle: God reveals that mature believers need to pass all their plans before God for the "how" of the fulfillment of His promises. God's work must be done God's way.

Abraham wanted to make sure he was **doing what he could** to realize the promise, so he checked with God on His plan to have heirs (15:2-3).

Genesis 15: 2 Abram said, "O Lord GOD, what will You give me, since I am childless, and the heir of my house is Eliezer of Damascus?" 3 And Abram said, "Since You have given no offspring to me, one born in my house is my heir."

The center of Abram's world was hollow. He saw God's promises and he believed God's person. The issue wasn't that God would not do great things for him, but rather that the promises God made seemed to fall short of what was really in his heart -- a groom wanted a child of his own. Abram had experienced incredible prosperity, yet the security of his heart was bound up in the desire to have a child or perhaps many children that would fill his later years with laughter and security. His words, "I am childless," echoes a hole inside.

Abraham wanted to please God but he was not sure how God would make good on His promise. As a result, he suggested that He should apply the typical custom of his day to answer the need. Abram spoke of his servant as his heir, when in fact he was not yet in need of an heir -- he was still alive and healthy. Wisely Abram posed the question to the Lord as to how He would fulfill His promise.

Herein is the inspection principle – mature believers aren't finished inquiring when they know what God wants. Mature believers need to know how God wants what He wants.

The fact of the matter is that many believers know what God wants in the long frame, but few of us understand what God is doing in the shorter frame. I think of this poignant story:

"Bruce Goodrich was being initiated into the cadet corps at Texas A & M University. One night, Bruce was forced to run until he dropped -- but he never got up. Bruce Goodrich died before he even entered college. A short time after the tragedy, Bruce's father wrote this letter to the administration, faculty, student body, and the corps of cadets:

"I would like to take this opportunity to express the appreciation of my family for the great outpouring of concern and sympathy from Texas A & M University and the college community over the loss of our son Bruce. We were deeply touched by the tribute paid to him in the battalion. We were particularly pleased to note that his Christian witness did not go unnoticed during his brief time on campus." Mr. Goodrich went on: "I hope it will be some comfort to know that we harbor no ill will in the matter. We know our God makes no mistakes. Bruce had an appointment with his Lord and is now secure in his celestial home. When the question is asked, 'Why did this happen?' perhaps one answer will be, 'So that many will consider where they will spend eternity.'" (*Our Daily Bread*, March 22, 1994)

What a response to the loss of a son! The truth is that a great testimony was given as much by the Goodrich family as by Bruce's life. We simply don't always get to understand in the here and now why God does what God does -- or how He is working.

Principle #3: Passive Principle: Because Abraham asked, he got God's direction.

Believers **need not fumble through life; we can ask God** for even a specific word of direction. God delights in our asking!

God responded to Abraham's query with a "No!" God told Abraham that He was going to meet the need in His own way (15:4-5).

Genesis 15:4 Then behold, the word of the LORD came to him, saying, "This man will not be your heir, but one who will come forth from your own body; he shall be your heir." 5 And He took him outside and said, "Now look toward the heavens, and count the stars, if you are able to count them." And He said to him, "So shall your descendants be."

Sometimes we need a **specific word** – not a general thing. I was moved when I read this:

"Jungle Aviation and Radio Service (JAARS), the flying department of Wycliffe Bible Translators, had flown thousands of hours over a 25 year span without one fatal accident before April 7, 1972. On that day, a Piper Aztec lost its right engine and crashed in Papua New Guinea, killing all seven persons aboard. The Aztec had just rolled out of the Wycliffe maintenance hangar the day before, following a 100 hour inspection.

The chief mechanic was stunned when he heard the news of the crash. Reviewing in his mind each step he had performed in inspecting that right engine, he suddenly recoiled in horror. He remembered that he had been interrupted while tightening a fuel line and had never returned to finish the job!

That faulty connection had allowed raw fuel to spray out and catch fire while the Aztec was in flight. The mechanic's guilt at being responsible for the deaths of his companions crushed him. For days he did not know what to do. The other mechanics tried to help him, as did his own family. But when the family of Doug Hunt, the pilot who was killed in the accident, was preparing to return to their home in New Zealand, the mechanic knew he had to see them, talk with them and beg their forgiveness. He could barely get out the words as he sobbed in their presence.

"That hand there," he said, looking at his right hand, "took Doug's life." Glennis Hunt, Doug's widow, embraced him.

"Glennis sat by me and held the hand that took her husband's life," he later wrote, "and another JAARS pilot sat on my other side with a demonstration of love, comfort, and forgiveness. That was the most significant first step in the healing process." (Max Lucado, *God Came Near*, Multnomah Press, 1987, p. 101)

The message of forgiveness could not be general – and it could not be from just anyone. It had meaning because of the PERSON and METHOD they used to communicate it.

Ask God to direct you. Ask God to explain about problems in your life. James 1 tells us to take the troubled circumstances of our lives to the throne room of God. **We need not fumble -- we can ask!**

Principle #4: Affirmation Principle: God's gifts come by His grace through the vehicle of our faith (simple acceptance and **acting on them as though they were already true**!).

Abraham accepted at face value God's promise, simply offering an "Amen!" to the plan. God accepted the simplicity of faith and set up the most intimate covenant with him, a covenant of blood (15:6-7).

Genesis 15: 6 Then he believed in the LORD; and He reckoned it to him as righteousness. 7 And He said to him, "I am the LORD Who brought you out of Ur of the Chaldeans, to give you this land to possess it."

Principle #5: Model Principle: God loves models! He shows us earthly things to mirror heavenly truths!

Abraham asked, "With what covenant symbol will you make this promise?" (15:8).

To close our story, note: God replied, "With blood!." (15:9-21)

15:9-21 So He said to him, "Bring Me a three year old heifer, and a three year old female goat, and a three year old ram, and a turtledove, and a young pigeon." 10 Then he brought all these to Him and cut them in two, and laid each half opposite the other; but he did not cut the birds. 11 The birds of prey came *down upon the carcasses, and Abram drove them away. 12 Now when the sun was going down, **a deep sleep fell upon Abram**; and behold, terror and great darkness fell upon him. 13 God said to Abram, "Know for certain that your descendants will be strangers in a land that is not theirs, where they will be enslaved and oppressed four hundred years. 14 But I will also judge the nation whom they will serve, and afterward they will come out with many possessions. 15 As for you, you shall go to your fathers in peace; you will be buried at a good old age. 16 Then in the fourth generation they will return here, for the iniquity of the Amorite is not yet complete." 17 It came about when the sun had set, that it was very dark, and behold, there appeared a smoking oven and a flaming torch which passed between these pieces. 18 On that day the LORD made a covenant with Abram, saying, "To your descendants I have given this land, from the river of Egypt as far as the great river, the river Euphrates: 19 the Kenite and the Kenizzite and the Kadmonite 20 and the Hittite and the Perizzite and the Rephaim 21 and the Amorite and the Canaanite and the Girgashite and the Jebusite."*

The covenant included new prophetic details:

- Your seed will be kept from the land, but return after four hundred years (13).
- They will be enslaved, but then set free by God (14).
- It will happen after your lifetime (15).
- God had a reason for this lapse (16).

Note that God made this covenant while Abraham slept. THE TERMS WERE NOT A MUTUAL AGREEMENT - IT WAS A UNILATERAL ONE! Abraham already offered consent by obediently killing the animals. **God's most intimate promises are given in blood covenant**. He made one with Abraham, but He also made one with us!

The terms of agreement with God are always **made BY GOD**. He alone can determine what is acceptable to Him. In our day, **ANOTHER BLOOD COVENANT** is offered - it is the blood of the Savior. The requirement is the same - **TO RECEIVE THE WORK OF GOD BY FAITH**. The work was in the blood covenant as the *Bible* says.

There are at least 43 references to the blood of Christ in the New Testament, all testifying to its great importance in the salvation and daily life of every believer. Here are some:

- Jesus started it all when he said, "This blood is the <u>new covenant</u> shed for many." (Matthew 26:28).
- Judas the betrayer spoke of it as <u>innocent blood</u> (Matthew 27:4)
- Peter called it the <u>precious blood</u> of Christ, as of a lamb without blemish and without spot (I Peter I:9).
- It is the <u>cleansing blood</u> in (1John 1:7).
- It is the <u>washing blood</u> in Rev. I:5, stressing that it removes the guilt of our sins.
- Paul calls it the <u>purchasing blood</u> in Acts 20:28
- Peter, Paul and John all call it the <u>redeeming blood</u> (Eph. I:7; Col. 1:14, I Peter I:18-19, Rev. 5:9)
- It is also the <u>justifying blood</u> -- declaring the shedding of His blood to be the very price of our salvation (Rom. 5:9)
- It is the <u>peacemaking blood</u> (Col. 1:20).
- It is also the <u>sanctifying blood</u> (Heb. 13:12).
- It is <u>holy blood</u> (Heb. 10:29),
- There is infinite and eternal power in the blood of Christ, for it is "the <u>blood of the everlasting covenant</u>" (Heb. 13:20).
- Yet, it is more. Revelation reminds us: And they <u>overcame Him by the blood</u> of the Lamb, and by the word of their testimony; and they loved not their lives unto the death (Rev. 12:11).

This is the last reference in the *Bible* to the shed blood of the Lord Jesus Christ; here it is the <u>overcoming blood</u>, enabling believers to withstand the deceptions and accusations of Satan.

The record of the New Testament is this -- the blood of Christ is:

- forever innocent,
- infinitely precious,
- perfectly justifying,
- always cleansing
- fully sanctifying,
- a powerful weapon to overcome the wicked one.

Following God's plan isn't "hocus pocus," but it requires thought, reflection and inspection - but it CAN BE KNOWN. The will of God in your life is not an "extra," it is essential, and God knows how to reveal it!

Reading the Map:
Lessons in Genesis

Lesson Fifteen: Genesis 16
"Helping Out God"

Over the last decade, Dr. Henry cloud and John Townsend have written a series of books that all begin with the word *"Boundaries."* In the original book by that name, the authors argued: "Confusion about responsibility and ownership in our lives is a problem of boundaries. Just as homeowners set physical property lines around their land, we need to set mental, physical, emotional, and spiritual boundaries for our lives to help us distinguish what is our responsibility and what isn't. Many sincere, dedicated believers struggle with tremendous confusion about what is biblically appropriate to set limits... Fences, signs, walls, notes with alligators, manicured lawns, where hedges are all physical boundaries. In their differing appearances, they give the same message: this is where my property begins. The owner of the property is legally responsible for what happens on his or her property. Non-owners are not responsible for the property. In the spiritual world, boundaries are just as real, but often harder to see... In reality, these boundaries define your soul, and they help you guard and maintain it." (Proverbs 4:23). (Boundaries: When to Say Yes, When to Say No, pages 8 – 12, 2004 edition)

Did you ever try to help God do something or which He gave you the goal, but you "filled in the blanks" on the HOW of it without asking Him? When we do this, we take God's place in our lives and violate the boundary between that which we are responsible for, and that which we alone can provide.

Abram and Sarai give us a great model of how NOT to help out God, with seven important observations in overcoming failure! God made promises four times to Abraham, and then delayed in fulfilling them. Anxious to have her husband experience all that God had promised, Sarah stepped in – and Abraham accepted her plan.

- Abraham had a full knowledge of the promises of God – the question was not **WHAT**, but **WHEN**!
- Abraham saw the faithfulness of God to him - the question was not **WHO**, but **HOW**!

Key Principle: When I seek to "help out" God by performing FOR Him, and not BY, THROUGH, and IN Him, I create a terrible mess out of His great promises!

Seven Observations on Overcoming Failure:

Observation One: Some are caused by our nature overcoming our walk with God. Sarah tried to fulfill God's promise (16:1). Following our natural desires to fulfill a role that God should fulfill will bring us pain, not fulfillment!

Genesis 16:1 "Now Sarai, Abram's wife had borne him no children, and she had an Egyptian maid whose name was Hagar.

Sara evaluated **three** inventory items: the **revelation** of God's will, her **inability** – what she didn't have or couldn't do, and what she did have – what she **controlled**. She missed a **fourth** inventory item – **her walk with God**.

At the root of our desire to step into God's role, we find impatience and fear. In his book fearless, Max Lucado writes in his work called "Fearless" about the power fear possesses to turn us into beastly people:

"Fear turns us into control freaks... Fear, at its center, is a perceived loss of control. When life spins wildly, we grab for a component of life we can manage: our diet, the tidiness of our home, the armrest of a plane, or, in many cases, people..."

That is so true! When we become afraid of things that are beyond our control, we compensate by grabbing onto things we think we can control. Control is an illusion. I cannot control the length of my life, the day of my death, and most events that will play into my life. My life is a stewardship exercise, and the truth is that God has only given me very limited parameters to control. The purpose of this is so that God can help me embrace my need of intimacy with Him.

Paul Stanley tells this story from his military experience:

"As an infantry company commander in Vietnam in 1967, I saw Viet Cong soldiers surrender many times. As they were placed in custody, marched away, and briefly interrogated, their body language and facial expressions always caught my attention. Most hung their heads in shame, staring at the ground, unwilling to look their captors in the eye. But some stood erect, staring defiantly at those around them, resisting any attempt by our men to control them. They had surrendered physically but not mentally.

On one occasion after the enemy had withdrawn, I came upon several soldiers surrounding a wounded Viet Cong. Shot through the lower leg, he was hostile and frightened, yet helpless. He threw mud and kicked with his one good leg when anyone came near him.

When I joined the circle around the wounded enemy, one soldier asked me, "Sir, what do we do? He's losing blood fast and needs medical attention."

I looked down at the struggling Viet Cong and saw the face of a 16 or 17-year-old boy. I unbuckled my pistol belt and hand grenades so he could not grab them. Then, speaking gently, I moved toward him. He stared fearfully at me as I knelt down, but he allowed me to slide my arms under him and pick him up.

As I walked with him toward a waiting helicopter, he began to cry and hold me tight. He kept looking at me and squeezing me tighter. We climbed into the helicopter and took off. During the ride, our young captive sat on the floor, clinging to my leg. Never having ridden in a helicopter, he looked out with panic as we gained altitude and flew over the trees. He fixed his eyes back on me, and I smiled reassuringly and put my hand on his shoulder.

After landing, I picked him up and walked toward the medical tent. As we crossed the field, I felt the tenseness leave his body and his tight grasp loosen. His eyes softened, and his head leaned against my chest. The fear and resistance were gone — he had finally surrendered." (sermon central illustrations).

Rev. Rodney Buchanan added these words to a message several years ago: That is the way it is when we surrender to God isn't it? At first we see God as the enemy and we fight Him, claiming our own territory and the right to our own lives. But in our woundedness, we finally see that we cannot conquer Him, and the God to whom we surrender is not our enemy. He cares for us and heals us as He takes us captive.

Observation Two: Some are caused by "misdirecting" our energy. Abraham was passive in the leadership of his home. (16:2). A failure to fulfill the role God currently has given you, will further delay God's blessing on your future roles and promises!

Genesis 16:2 So Sarai said to Abram, "Now behold, the LORD has prevented me from bearing children. Please go in to my maid; perhaps I will obtain children through her." And Abram listened to the voice of Sarai.

Sarai did not see that **God's work was God's responsibility** to complete. She could do her part, but **He alone could bring about the result**. When we don't understand the part that is ours to do, and rest in the part that is NOT ours to do, we misdirect our energy. We worry or we work in an area we are not called to work.

Worry is a function of disappointment with God's appointed or delayed result. Wrong work is a function of poor boundaries with God – rooted in discontentment. God has a way of taking care of things that are His to do. When we go beyond the boundary into His work, even when we think we are so smart, we set ourselves up for deep disappointment.

I heard about a young lawyer who was called in from the big city to represent a large railroad company that was being sued by a farmer. It seems that the farmer's prize cow was missing from a field through which the railroad passed, and the farmer was suing for the value of the cow. Before the case was to be tried, the lawyer cornered the farmer and convinced him to settle out of court for half of what he originally wanted. The farmer signed the necessary papers and then accepted the check.

The young lawyer could not resist gloating a bit about his success. He said to the farmer, "You know, I couldn't have won this case if it had gone to trial. The engineer was asleep and the fireman was in the caboose when the train passed through your farm that morning. I didn't have a single witness to put on the stand!"

With a wry smile, the old farmer replied, "Well, I tell you young feller, I was a little worried about winning that case myself because that cow came home this morning." (Rev. Mark Peake, Sermon Central.com illustrations)

Observation Three: All failures are enhanced by flesh performance. Neither Abraham nor Sarah consulted God in their plan (16:3-4). A believer can do what "feels right" or will "seem to work" and create greater pain and trouble!

Genesis 16:3 After Abram had lived ten years in the land of Canaan, Abram's wife Sarai took Hagar the Egyptian, her maid, and gave her to her husband Abram as his wife. 4 He went in to Hagar and she conceived; and when Hagar saw that she had conceived, her mistress (Sarai) was despised in her sight.

Sarai hatched a plan that **left her feeling worse when it succeeded!** When we work outside of God's plan, we will expend our energies trying to solve problems that are His to solve, and we will rely on the tiniest resources of the flesh – not the vast and powerful resources of God. The results left her less powerful, less in control – less certain. In the end, she empowered another with her actions, and Hagar was able to "take lightly" (vat·te·kal, from qawlal, or lightened) her mistress. She was now important and able to feel indispensable. Never before empowered, Hagar misused the power.

One of the most dangerous things we can do in the process of belly flopping into failure is to drag in other people who are unprepared for the circumstance, and set them up to fail alongside us. Once this happens, we damage the relationship and most times, apart from the Lord, we can never recover it.

Observation Four: Failures cannot be overcome without identifying the real underlying problem.
Neither Abraham nor Sarah detected the **true problem when troubles materialized (16:5-6). The underlying deception** must be rooted out to truly solve the problem!

Genesis 16:5 And Sarai said to Abram, "May the wrong done me be upon you. I gave my maid into your arms, but when she saw that she had conceived, I was despised in her sight. May the LORD judge between you and me." 6 But Abram said to Sarai, "Behold, your maid is in your power; do to her what is good in your sight." So Sarai treated her harshly, and she fled from her presence.

Once Sarai took God's role to supply what God alone should have been called upon to do, she realized the problem of playing God – things aren't really in your control! Things, in fact, got worse. She lost control over the servant she once felt secure in controlling. Faced with insult and feeling rejected (because of her own choice not to seek God), she blamed Abram, driving him further away. She tried to make Abram responsible for the reaction of Hagar – still misdirecting energy and misunderstanding the boundaries.

Abram attempted to quell the problem by reminding Sarai that her position visa vie the slave Hagar was unchanged. He took his hands off – because passivity was his trademark in his family. He did not oversee the household, nor did he point out error. He didn't even attempt to direct her back to God. He was too busy to protect her from herself.

Observation Five: Many (not just ME!) suffer from my failures. Hagar ended up stripped of her dignity, despised and on the run (16:7).

Wrong assumptions and poor choices lead to victimization in those who were not a part of our problem - until we dragged them in.

Genesis 16:7 Now the angel of the LORD found her by a spring of water in the wilderness, by the spring on the way to Shur. 8 He said, "Hagar, Sarai's maid, where have you come from and where are you going?" And she said, "I am fleeing from the presence of my mistress Sarai."

Sarai dragged in Hagar to a problem that Hagar had nothing to do with. In the world the solution was simple, but without seeking God this was a **guess**, not a certain step of faith. It was taking a **partial revelation** and "filling in the blanks" without seeking Him concerning those blanks.

When we jump too fast and without asking, we jump badly – and the plunge affects many! Add to the fact that not only did Abram not stop and direct his wife (but went in to Hagar), he did not stop to consider the ramifications of what he was doing. He placed Hagar in a privileged position without preparation, and she predictably mishandled herself. He placed his wife in a place open to jealousy. When he was given opportunity to rectify the wrong, he dropped the situation back in his wife's lap. When it blew up, (the first on hundreds of thousands of blow-ups in this family!) he let injustice grow. There was no discussion about the baby, there was only a deafening silence from the leader of the clan, and the sound of a pregnant woman's footsteps leaving the camp...

How many have suffered over the ages because of the lack of direction from Abram?

Observation Six: God is not afraid of stepping in to failure scenarios. The angel directed Hagar's return (16:8-9). The beginning of blessing is submission to God's Word!

Genesis 16:9 Then the angel of the LORD said to her, "Return to your mistress, and submit yourself to her authority."

Hagar left to the place at the edge of life. She was done, and had no place to turn. The one God had given to her to take responsibility (Abram) refused to do so. The woman appointed to be directly over her pushed her away. Alone, broken and running away, she too failed to take the matter to the God who promised to superintend the whole family.

God stepped in without being asked PRECISELY BECAUSE He was not being asked. He wanted to work a plan, but no one seemed to think they should ask Him about how the plan was to work! He came with a question of His own. It was the question He was no doubt asking through the whole story to everyone in it – "Where are you going?"

Observation Seven: God does see the inequities, and is able to put something great together even in the midst of pain. Hagar received promises that encouraged her (16:10-16). God builds up, even standing with us in the dump of all the destruction we have experienced on our way to Him!

Genesis 16:10 Moreover, the angel of the LORD said to her, "I will greatly multiply your descendants so that they will be too many to count." 11 The angel of the LORD said to her further, "Behold, you are with child, and you will bear a son; and you shall call his name Ishmael, because the LORD has given heed to your affliction. 12 He will be a wild donkey of a man, his hand will be against everyone, and everyone's hand will be against him; and he will live to the east of all his brothers." 13Then she called the name of the LORD who spoke to her, "You are a God Who sees"; for she said, "Have I even remained alive here after seeing Him?" 14 Therefore the well was called Beer-lahai-roi; behold, it is between Kadesh and Bered. 15 So Hagar bore Abram a son; and Abram called the name of his son, whom Hagar bore, Ishmael. 16 Abram was eighty-six years old when Hagar bore Ishmael to him.

I want to lay aside the notion that in this text an Arab is somehow cursed by the words spoken of Ishmael and his generations in Genesis 16:12, (as some of our erring brethren have implied in their writings):

And he will be a wild man (literally "wild ass"); **his hand will be against every man, and every man's hand against him; and he shall dwell in the presence of all his brethren.**

I truly believe that a closer examination of the Genesis promise about Ishmael will reveal that there is NO curse of Ishmael. I do not believe the verse says ANYTHING NEGATIVE about

Ishmael and his descendants. On the contrary, when you look carefully, Hagar left because she
could not bear the mistreatment of Sarai. The angel of the Lord came to her and promised her some **great things** if she would return and submit to the difficult treatment.

- First, he said that God would multiply her seed into a **multitude**.
- Second, he told her that she would have a **son** (presumably through which the first promise would be accomplished) – and that she was to call the child "Ishmael" (Literally "God hears").
- Third, she heard about the **blessing** of this child.

The blessing was in three parts:

1) He would be a "**wild ass**". At the time of the prophecy, Hagar saw wealth in terms of herds of camels, goats, sheep and donkeys. The nomadic life was not unlike the Bedouin today, a life of travel. The better pack animals were expensive, but necessary for moving. The onacker (wild ass) is the kind left to wander and breed in the donkeys to add strength. It was an expensive animal, somewhat rare and very sought after. The promise, I believe was simple: your son will be an admired and valuable asset.

2) The phrase "**his hand will be against every man**" is probably better translated more literally. The Hebrew of the passage reads: "*YADO B'KOL V' YAD KOL BO..*" A literal reading of the passage says: *His hand in everything and hand everything (in)...* The translation has been taken as a negative, "*His hand will be against every man*", but is not the only way to read the passage. I wonder why an angel would try to encourage a mother with words like, "Everyone will be against your child!" It seems strange. I think the promise was also economic, and matches the end of the verse. I would suggest the meaning to be, "His hands will be in everything, and mixed with many others" as in "He will be an enterprising youngster!" What could you say to a mother that would be more encouraging than "**Your child will be wise in business!**"

3) The final phrase bears out this translation. The final phrase is translated in some versions, "He shall **dwell in the presence** of all of his brothers" (KJV) or "he shall live east (before the face of) of his brothers" (NAS). I suspect that both were to be true, but it seems like the issue of the text is the opportunities of the child.

If he would be a "valuable young man, and his hands would be well mixed in the economy of his brothers," the final phrase was probably meant to assure her of "his ability to live among his brothers" (as opposed to her feeling that she must flee the tents of Abraham!).

At the end of the day, **we control nothing but the yielded door within of our own heart** before the Lord.   We cannot move others.   We cannot bring about great events   We can yield ourselves continually to God, and that is ALL we can do. We often help out God because we cannot understand the boundaries and purposes of God.

Pastor Wayne Hughes, Sr. tells the story: I have been pondering a story of a weak sickly man. The man was so sick but he could not afford going to town to the doctor. The man lived in the deep back woods in an old log cabin; his condition seemed to grow worse. Out in front of his cabin was a huge boulder. The rock was massive in front of his place. One night in a very real vision, God told him to go out there and push the huge rock all day long, day after day. The man got up early in the morning, and with great excitement he pushed the rock until lunch, then he rested a while and pushed the rock until supper time. The man loved pushing against the rock; it gave him meaning. The dream was so real that it was with great excitement he pushed against the rock.

Day after day he pushed. Day rolled into week, and week into months, he faithfully pushed against the rock. After 8 months of pushing the rock, the weak sickly man was getting tired of pushing the rock so much. In his tiredness he started to doubt his dream.

So one day he measured from his porch to the rock, and after daily pushing the rock, he would measure to see how much he had moved the rock. After two weeks of pushing and measuring, he realized he had not moved the boulder, not a 1/32 of an inch! As a matter of fact, the boulder was in the same place as when he started. The man was so disappointed; he thought the dream was so special and now after 9 months he saw his work had accomplished nothing. He was tired and his dream seemed dashed upon the rock. The man sat on his porch and cried and cried. He had invested many hundreds of hours into nothing. Nothing, it was all nothing!

As the sun was sitting in the west, Jesus came and sat down next to the man as he cried. Jesus said, "Son, why are you crying?" The man replied, "Lord, You know how sick and weak I am, and then this dumb dream gave me a false hope and I have pushed with all that was within me for over 9 months, and that dumb old rock is right where it was when I started." Jesus was kind and said to him, "I never told you to move the rock, I told you to push against the rock." The man replied, "Yes, Sir, that was the dream."

Jesus told the man to step in front of the mirror and look at himself. As an act of obedience the man stepped in front of a mirror and looked at himself. The once sickly man was now quite strengthened by his labors. Muscles that once had atrophied were now fully developed. It was only then the man began to understand that Jesus did not want him to move the rock, He wanted the rock to sculpt the man's body." (*Sermon Central*.com *Illustrations*)

When we seek to "help out" God by performing FOR Him, and not BY, THROUGH and IN Him, we create a terrible mess out of His great promises!

Reading the Map:
Lessons in Genesis

Lesson Sixteen: Genesis 17:1-16
"The Terms of God's Blessing"

We started some sixteen chapters ago to explore the foundational principles of God's Word in the opening book of Moses. At the time that we began the study, we posited the idea that God laid some foundational principles in the opening of His Word. We saw that when we dig a deep foundation into the word of God, we build a strong and stable structure in our lives. By the middle of Chapter 11 of Genesis, we followed the story to Abram. If his life has any one single word attached to it in the Bible-- that word would be **blessing**.

As we continue our study, I want to talk to you about blessing -- and more specifically what terms God places on receiving His blessing. For a believer, there is **perhaps no more compelling question then this: "Am I walking in the path of God's blessing?"**

- She sits alone waiting for the phone to ring. She knows that God has good things for her; she has prayed and read her *Bible*. What now? Is there a way that God can open His hand to her sense of loneliness?

- He recognizes that he is done many things wrong in his life. He has surrendered to the Lord, and asked Jesus to make his life anew. Each night he comes home from work to an empty house, empty since he drove his wife and children away. Is there any way for a new start to come to his life? He cannot go back and change the past -- can he meet the terms of God for blessing in his future?

Is there a path to blessing? People everywhere around us seem to be needy and unfulfilled. **Does God reveal markers of the journey to blessing in the *Bible*?** The answer is **YES!**

Consider again Abraham's story. With the birth of Ishmael, God waited at least another thirteen years to move in and fulfill His promises to Abraham! We glimpse into the story of Abraham at age 99, as God moves powerfully one more time, changing his name and setting in motion the long-awaited promise.

Key Principle: An open heart to revealed truth leads to solid belief and obedient steps. These steps lead to fulfillment of one's deepest longings and desires.

The Foundation of Blessing is a life surrendered to the revealed truth of God (17:1-2).

Abram's life can be summarized by a series of meetings with God that were followed by a demonstrative surrender of his life and his goals -- conforming his life in trust to God's Word. Abram's daily living was impacted by God's revealed standard in his life!

- **Emptying Promise**: The first meeting was in Genesis 12:1-3, when God told Abram to move out to a country God would show him, and that God would make Abram a blessing to all nations.

- **Defined Land Promise**: The second meeting was recorded in 12:7 when God told Abram that he would receive all the land he could see for his descendants.

- **Extended Time Promise**: Another meeting was recorded in 13:14, after Abraham rescued lot and gave tithes to Melchisedek. God promised Abraham the land allotment would be forever his for his family.

- **Specified Lineage Promise**: This fourth meeting between God and Abraham was the record of a vision where God made an additional promise: Your household will have great reward. Abram asks "How?" God replies, "Your seed will be many, and come from YOU!" 15:1ff.

- **Matriarchal Promise**: I will raise up your seed through Sarah, and not through Hagar as the primary recipient of my eternal blessing (17:1ff).

Genesis 17:1 Now when Abram was ninety-nine years old, the LORD appeared to Abram and said to him, "I am God Almighty (El Shaddai); walk before Me, and be blameless (tawmim). 2 "I will establish My covenant between Me and you, And I will multiply you exceedingly."

We have seen it before, God meeting with Abram to give him further revelation about the promises that would be his and his children's after him. In this text, El Shaddai called Abram and told him to appear for divine inspection (17:1) so that God could bestow His promised blessing of children (17:2).

Note **three principles** that are demonstrated in this meeting:

- **Patience principle**: God took his time getting to Abraham some vital parts of the plan. Abram was 99 years old in our story, suggesting that God was in no hurry to reveal all aspects of His will. That being the case, believers should understand that God may reveal His desire for them slowly over a long period of time. We need to become more patient -- letting God be God in our lives (17:1).

- **Personality principle**: As God revealed Himself carefully over Abram's lifetime, the patriarch learned more about God's character, and God's nature. Part of the purpose of delays in our life must be to deepen our understanding of God Himself. Note that God used here a title *El Shaddai* which is translated God Almighty. If God simply made promises to us, and then met all of our promises in short order, we would learn much less of Him -- and we would not learn to trust Him well. God whispers in our successes but screams in our pain. Patiently waiting on Him helps us understand Him in deeper ways (17:1b).

- **Purity principle**: When God called upon Abram, He told him to walk in front of Him for inspection, and to come into that place without spot or blemish. God deeply desired to bless Abram, but blemishes and spots hold back the Father's hand from bringing such blessing. God will not risk teaching us in a wrong way, and cannot condone rebellion by rewarding us (17:2a).

The Attitude of Blessing is a reverent heart (17:3).

I am convinced now more than ever that our view of God -- His nature, His might, and His holiness -- are largely the determining factors of the blessing of our life. When we do not view God as He is, we do not view life properly. We become too large in our own eyes -- and He becomes too small. When we reverence Him, when we feel fortunate just to stand before Him in His presence, then our hearts are aligned with truth in a way that opens us to His blessing.

How do I know that my heart is truly bowing in His presence? I know it by the submission of my hands and feet. "When the heart is right, the feet are swift!" When God calls, and my heart is right before Him, I find little resistance in my spirit to humbling myself before Him. Without the need to prepare himself further, Abram came immediately into God's presence in worship.

Genesis 17:3 Abram fell on his face, and God talked with him...

The words of Eleanor Roosevelt ring true: **One's philosophy is not best expressed in words. It is expressed in the choices one makes.**

The Conditions of Blessing includes obedience steps (17:4-8).

God saw Abram's **heart**, and met his **needs** with Divine power. God's blessings were specifically tailored, and follow **six important principles** (17:4-8):

Principle One: They are *Deliberate*: I chose you out of the many (17:4). God encourages by letting His followers know that they are not a random accident, but a choice of love.

17:4 As for Me, behold, My covenant is with you.

Principle Two: They are *Impacting*: I will use you to affect millions (17:4b) and they will know you by your new name (17:5-6). God affirms how profound an obedient believer affects his whole world!

Genesis 17:4-6 And you will be the father of a multitude of nations. 5 No longer shall your name be called Abram, but your name shall be Abraham, for I have made you the father of a multitude of nations. 6 I will make you exceedingly fruitful, and I will make nations of you, and kings will come forth from you.

Understanding is the reward of faith. Therefore, seek not to understand that thou mayest believe, but believe that thou mayest understand. Augustine

Principle Three: They are *Intimate*: I will maintain the covenant through the generations after you are gone (17:7). God reaches into the life of a follower to fulfill their deepest longings!

Genesis 17:7 I will establish My covenant between Me and you and your descendants after you throughout their generations for an everlasting covenant, to be God to you and to your descendants after you.

God knows how to show us, through a series of practical life experiences, the facts about His abilities and His nature. We don't really believe in a God we do not live for!

In college I was asked to prepare a lesson to teach my speech class. We were to be graded on our creativity and ability to drive home a point in a memorable way. The title of my talk was, "The Law of the Pendulum." I spent 20 minutes carefully teaching the physical principle that governs a swinging pendulum.

The law of the pendulum is: A pendulum can never return to a point higher than the point from which it was released.

Because of friction and gravity, when the pendulum returns, it will fall short of its original release point. Each time it swings it makes less and less of an arc, until finally it is at rest. This point of rest is called the state of equilibrium, where all forces acting on the pendulum are equal. I attached a 3-foot string to a child's toy top and secured it to the top of the blackboard with a thumbtack. I pulled the top to one side and made a mark on the blackboard where I let it go. Each time it swung back I made a new mark. It took less than a minute for the top to complete its swinging and come to rest. When I finished the demonstration, the markings on the blackboard proved my thesis.

I then asked how many people in the room BELIEVED the law of the pendulum was true. All of my classmates raised their hands, so did the teacher. He started to walk to the front of the room thinking the class was over. In reality it had just begun.

Hanging from the steel ceiling beams in the middle of the room was a large, crude but functional pendulum (250 pounds of metal weights tied to four strands of 500-pound test parachute cord.). I invited the instructor to climb up on a table and sit in a chair with the back of his head against a cement wall. Then I brought the 250 pounds of metal up to his nose. Holding the huge pendulum just a fraction of an inch from his face, I once again explained the law of the pendulum he had applauded only moments before, "If the law of the pendulum is true, then when I release this mass of metal, it will swing across the room and return short of the release point. Your nose will be in no danger."

After that final restatement of this law, I looked him in the eye and asked, "Sir, do you believe this law is true?" There was a long pause. Huge beads of sweat formed on his upper lip and then weakly he nodded and whispered, "Yes."

I released the pendulum. It made a swishing sound as it arced across the room. At the far end of its swing, it paused momentarily and started back. I never saw a man move so fast in my life. He literally dived from the table.

Deftly stepping around the still-swinging pendulum, I asked the class, "Does he believe in the law of the pendulum?"

The students unanimously answered, "NO!"   (Ken Davis, *How To Speak To Youth*, pp. 104-106)

Reading the Map: Lessons in Genesis

Principle Four: They build *Confidence*: I will meet your physical needs and be a guardian to your children (17:8). God secures the heart of His follower concerning their deepest worries!

Genesis 17:8 I will give to you and to your descendants after you, the land of your sojournings, all the land of Canaan, for an everlasting possession; and I will be their God.

You never know how much you really believe anything until its truth or falsehood becomes a matter of life and death. It is easy to say you believe a rope to be strong as long as you are merely using it to cord a box. But suppose you had to hang by that rope over a precipice. Wouldn't you then first discover how much you really trusted it? (C.S. Lewis, *A Grief Observed*)

F.E. Marsh has enumerated some of God's blessings:

- An acceptance that can never be questioned (Ephesians 1:6).
- An inheritance that can never be lost (I Peter 1:3-5).
- A deliverance that can never be excelled (2 Corinthians I:10).
- A grace that can never be limited (2 Corinthians 12:9).
- A hope that can never be disappointed (Hebrews 6:18, 19).
- A bounty that can never be withdrawn (I Colossians 3:21-23).
- A joy that need never be diminished. (John 15:11).
- A nearness to God that can never be reversed (Ephesians 2:13).
- A peace that can never be disturbed (John 14:27).
- A righteousness that can never be tarnished (2 Corinthians 5:21).
- A salvation that can never be canceled (Hebrews 5:9).

Principle Five: They are *Prescribed*. I will set the requirements for following Me (17:9-14).

*Genesis 17:9 God said further to Abraham, "Now as for you, you shall **keep My covenant**, you and your descendants after you* *throughout their generations. 10 This is My covenant, which you shall keep, between Me and you and your descendants after you: every male among you shall be **circumcised**. 11 And you shall be circumcised in the flesh of your foreskin, and it shall be the sign of the covenant between Me and you. 12 And every male among you who is **eight days old** shall be circumcised throughout your generations, a **servant** who is born in the house or who is bought with money from any foreigner, who is not of your descendants. 13 A servant who is born in your house or who is bought with your money shall surely be circumcised; thus shall My covenant be in your flesh for an everlasting covenant. 14 But an **uncircumcised** male who is not circumcised in the flesh of his foreskin, that person shall be **cut off from his people**; he has broken My covenant.*

God set the standards of obedience in His follower's lives for each generation! The standard of God included several specifics:

- The covenant was to be kept by each succeeding generation.

- The covenant was to be marked by the circumcision of each eight-day-old male.

- The covenant was to be expressed in the circumcision of both the household and servants -- whether born within the family, were bought from abroad.

- The covenant symbol was absolute, and failure to maintain the standard was punished by banishment.

Symbols have importance in the passing of the torch of blessing.

"At age 16 Andor Foldes was already a skilled pianist, but he was experiencing a troubled year. In the midst of the young Hungarian's personal struggles, one of the most renowned pianists of the day came to Budapest.

Emil von Sauer was famous not only for his abilities; he was also the last surviving pupil of the great Franz Liszt. Von Sauer requested that Foldes play for him. Foldes obliged with some of the most difficult works of Bach, Beethoven, and Schumann. When he finished, Von Sauer walked over to him and kissed him on the forehead.

"My son," he said, "when I was your age I became a student of Liszt. He kissed me on the forehead after my first lesson, saying, 'Take good care of this kiss--it comes from Beethoven, who gave it to me after hearing me play.' I have waited for years to pass on this sacred heritage, but now I feel you deserve it." (*Source Unknown*)

Principle Six: They are *Overflowing*: I will change the identity of your partner (17:15) and bless her because of your faith (17:16). God blesses the people around us because of our right response to His love and His Word!

Genesis 17:15-16 Then God said to Abraham, "As for Sarai your wife, you shall not call her name Sarai, but Sarah shall be her name. 16 I will bless her, and indeed I will give you a son by her. Then I will bless her, and she shall be a mother of nations; kings of peoples will come from her."

One morning R.C. Chapman, a devout Christian, was asked how he was feeling. "I'm burdened this morning!" was his reply. But his happy countenance contradicted his words.

So the questioner exclaimed in surprise, "Are you really burdened, Mr. Chapman?"

"Yes, but it's a wonderful burden--it's an overabundance of blessings for which I cannot find enough time or words to express my gratitude!"

Seeing the puzzled look on the face of his friend, Chapman added with a smile, "I am referring to Psalm 68:19, which fully describes my condition. In that verse the Father in Heaven reminds us that He 'daily loads us with benefits.'" (*Sermon Central Illustrations*).

I was moved by some of the titles in the new book The Christian Atheist. It is an interesting book written by a Christian author to challenge believers who are not living the truth of what they say they believe. Some of it has interesting chapter titles are these:

- When you believe in God but don't really know Him Chapter 1
- When you believe in God but you are shamed of your past -- Chapter 2
- When you believe in God but aren't sure He loves you - Chapter 3
- When you believe in God but not in prayer -- Chapter 4
- When you believe in God but don't think He's fair -- Chapter 5
- When you believe in God but won't forget -- Chapter 6
- When you believe in God but don't think you can change -- Chapter 7
- When you believe in God but still worry all the time -- Chapter 8
- When you believe in God but pursue happiness at any cost -- Chapter 9
- When you believe in God but trust more in money -- Chapter 10
- When you believe in God but don't share your faith -- Chapter 11
- When you believe in God but not in His church -- Chapter 12

These titles suggest that at least some believers are walking around saying they believe in a God they neither trust nor reverence. Their heart is closed, and their steps are disobedient. Sadly, many are probably wondering why they are not experiencing blessing.

What were the terms of blessing? An open heart to revealed truth that leads to firm trust and obedient steps equals **blessing**!

Consider these words: "When the author walks onto the stage, the play is over. God is going to invade, all right; but what is the good of saying you are on His side then, when you see the whole natural universe melting away like a dream and something else comes crashing in? This time it will be God without disguise, something so overwhelming that it will strike either irresistible love or irresistible horror into every creature. It will be too late then to choose your side. That will not be the time for choosing; it will be the time when we discover which side we really have chosen, whether we realized it before or not. Now, today, this moment, is our chance to choose the right side." (C.S. Lewis.)

Reading the Map: Lessons in Genesis

Reading the Map:
Lessons in Genesis

Lesson Seventeen: Genesis 17:17-18:16
"The Mother of All Blessing"

This lesson gives us an opportunity to especially focus on Sarah, and the work God did in and through her. It would be suitable for a "Mother's Day" focus, but we should be thinking through this incredibly important role all of the year – that of a mom.

Pastor Joe McKeever wrote: Why is it so difficult for pastors of all ages to preach Mother's Day sermons? My hunch is it has nothing to do with faulty relationships with their mothers. It has more to do with two realities: a) They do not want to go all sentimental and just preach a "How Wonderful is Motherhood" sermon, and yet are not clear what to do; and b) They are mostly men. My granddaughter was the one who reminded me of this. I was pushing my 8-year-old granddaughter Abby in the swing in her front yard, our favorite place. She and her twin Erin had been learning about childbirth from their mother. Abby was not liking what she was learning.

"I'm not going to have children, Grandpa," she said. "It hurts too bad." My first thought was to say, "If your mother felt that way, you would not be here. And if your great-grandmothers felt that way, none of us would be here." But what I said was, "You're right. It does hurt. But the pain goes away, and you're left with this beautiful child, and you decide that it was worth it." The child looked me square in the eyes and said, "You're a man. What do you know?" After picking myself up off the grass, I laughingly admitted she was exactly right—all I know on this subject is what I've been taught. Let us admit the obvious here: This is one experience where we men are on the outside looking in. We men are out of our league trying to assess what mothers go through and the challenges they face. (Sermon Central illustrations).

Now that I have admitted my obvious lack, let's take a look at Genesis 18 -- the woman behind the man. For some women in our modern world it seems difficult to remember the vital role that she plays in preserving the future... Kids get it, they know who holds the family together in so many homes. I remember the story about the teacher who gave a quiz to her students about magnets.

"After spending a class the day before talking about magnetism, she was surprised when she offered a quiz. The simple question she asked was this: "My name has six letters, I begin with "M", and I pick things up. Who am I?" The teacher was shocked to find that over 50% of her students filled in the answer as "mother."

Some of the greatest men in history will tell you how important their mothers were to their lives.

George Washington, for example, declared: **"All I am I owe to my mother."**

Obviously, to many of us, our mothers were a critical link to the Lord Himself.

The *Christian Herald* ran the story years ago of a Confederate chaplain who was visiting with a wounded solider. When it came time to pray, the chaplain was surprised that the wounded soldier did not make the usual request which was to petition God for a speedy recovery. The request was a prayer of thankfulness for his mother -- praise and gratitude to God for giving him a Christian mother who had so much influence in his life that she caused him to consider Christ. He praised the Lord that God enabled him to appreciate the sacrifice his mother made for him in prayer, making sure that he had the teaching of God's Word and especially for living a God-fearing life.

Not long after the prayer of praise, the soldier died. However, before the soldier died he asked the chaplain to contact his mother and be sure to let her know he died a Christian.

Our children will face many battles that threaten their walk. Therefore, they need mothers who have a Biblical influence -- and their importance cannot be underestimated.

In recent weeks we have been studying about blessing from Abraham's perspective, but God's work was to bless **his wife** as well. **God's work in Sarah was not incidental, and her obedience and surrender was not a small thing.** On the face of the narrative, she looked like a "**background player.**"

Many women feel like that today – behind their husband, behind their children. Laundry sponsor, soccer pickup taxi – it is hard to feel significant in such a role.

Key Principle: My surrender to God as a mom is vital to the blessing of my family, and the future of my heritage.

God will bless you with glimpses of His glory for that surrender.

Seven Truths about the Vital Role of Godly Mothers:

Truth 1: COVERING PRINCIPLE – A godly mother must recognize that God reveals His plan most clearly when those He has placed over us listen to Him.

*Genesis 17:15 Then God said to Abraham, "As for Sarai your wife, you shall not call her name Sarai, but Sarah shall be her name. 16 I will bless her, and indeed I will give you a son **by her**. Then **I will bless her**, and she shall be a mother of nations; kings of peoples will come from her."*

It is a hindrance to your role if those who "covered" you were not right with God. It doesn't mean that YOU CANNOT FOLLOW God; it means you didn't hear God's plan when you should have. Don't use that as an excuse, but let it be a warning as you care for others – they need you to follow God so that you will help them on THEIR journey!

You see, God revealed His plan for Sarah to Abraham before He did it to her (17:15). Abraham was responsible to impart that knowledge and undergird trust in God's Word. If God called Abraham to grow the foundation of a nation that would serve Him, God also called her.

Remember: **God will not call a man to go where He has not called his wife to go**.

Recently my daughter and I were talking about those "who have never met God." She was trying to figure out how God could expect people from countries that did not follow Him to learn of Him.

"Biblically," I said, "they all came from families that knew God at one time. Everyone left the ark together!"

In other words, it is easy to forget that **at some point, someone chose to walk away from the faith of their fathers, and taught their children to do the same**.

If there is any truth that is under-taught in our society, it is the truth of "boundaries and coverings." I want to take a minute to talk about these, not to leave our text, but because the problem of the text is rooted in this very issue. Too often I am finding people who are trying their absolute hardest in relationships and are exhausted and defeated. They are putting in the effort, and trying harder is not the problem. Very often, I find the problem is that even mature believers fail to draw a line between "what is mine to care for" and "what is someone else's to care for."

For example, it is not uncommon in our day to find some children who managed to get to be 25 years old or even 30 years old, and still depend on mom and dad for significant support. There are always the exceptional children, (I have an autistic brother) but more often than not we find an irresponsible and happy child being supported by unduly responsible and miserable parents.

This is essentially a **boundary and covering issue**. When we do not draw lines around our relationships in harmony with God's principles about them, we find ourselves frustrated.

Yet, if you look carefully at Jesus' relationship with His Father, Jesus understood that His Father was responsible to care for things for which Jesus bore no responsibility. At the same time, Jesus understood His responsibility before His Father.

In our story, Abraham had every responsibility to "cover" his wife by sharing with her what God said to him. He had the responsibility to help her trust God. Failure to do so, left her open to later sin by lacking trust in God when the revelation came to her, and then lying to cover her lack of belief. Abraham was being passive as Adam was before him. In both cases, failure to cover led to tragedy.

Believers must understand where their boundaries are, and where the coverings that God is put in place are, so that they may serve Him well, and cause those around them to serve Him well.

Sarah's faith was a reflection of her husband's weakness to prepare her for God's great work (cp. 18:12).

Truth 2: EXPANSION PRINCIPLE – A godly mother must believe that God will make more of your life than you can be apart from Him (17:17).

If there is one thing every believer should know is this: "Don't judge a book's potential by its current place on the charts."

We have all become much more because of the touch of God in our lives. He took broken vessels and made whole lives. In many cases, He did it by calling us to follow Him by faith, even when it did not match the worldview we had when we met Him.

Look closely at verse 17: Then Abraham fell on his face and laughed, and said in his heart, "Will a child be born to a man one hundred years old? And will Sarah, who is ninety years old, bear a child?" 18 And Abraham said to God, "Oh that Ishmael might live before You!"

- When you look carefully at these verses, you can see two important details:

- God may call you to **live truths beyond common experience** and conventional logic (17:17).

- It may be **beyond the desires** of those around you (17:18).

Note that both of these details include the word "beyond." God has a plan for us. His Word reveals that plan will take us in directions farther than we could ever imagine. One of the great responsibilities of a parent is to keep in mind that a child can become, if yielded to Jesus, much more than we see. We dare not hold them back, but should look for ways to see God's hand at work in their lives beyond the norm.

Many of those who God used in Scripture were reminded of God's call from before they were even conscious. The Jewish people heard from the mouth of the prophet Jeremiah the word of God.

Jeremiah 29:10 For thus says the LORD, "When seventy years have been completed for Babylon, I will visit you and fulfill My good word to you, to bring you back to this place. 11 'For I know the plans that I have for you,' declares the LORD, 'plans for welfare and not for calamity to give you a future and a hope. 12 Then you will call upon Me and come and pray to Me, and I will listen to you.'"

Much later, Paul celebrated God's divine choosing and planning in Ephesians: *1:3 Blessed be the God and Father of our Lord Jesus Christ, Who has blessed us with every spiritual blessing in the heavenly places in Christ, 4 just as He chose us in Him before the foundation of the world, that we would be holy and blameless before Him…*

Over and over the Scripture reveals that God plans for His children -- they are not a mistake or an afterthought. Not only does he plan for us to know Him, but He plans to expand as well beyond the boundaries of anything we could ever have accomplished without Him!

Truth 3: EXCHANGE PRINCIPLE – A godly mother must grasp that God will replace surrendered doubt with laughter and surrendered longing with joy (17:19). God takes what we yield to Him, and uses it to tell HIs story. In the end, it is most healthy, deeply enriching and joyful thing we can do!

*Genesis 17:19 But God said, "**No**, but **Sarah** your wife will bear you a son, and you shall call his name Isaac; and I will establish My covenant with him for an everlasting covenant for his descendants after him."*

The key to blessing is surrender. Though we can **influence** others, but we cannot **change** them. Yet, conversely, we are responsible to **yield ourselves** to God, that He may change us.

Why do we spend so much time griping about change in others while we are slack on changes in ourselves?

God says: *Charm is deceitful and beauty is passing, but a woman who reveres the Lord will be praised* (Proverbs 31:30).

When we do so, we open the door of His blessing on us, our family, and those all about us.

Now look closer at God's blessings: **His blessing may come by giving us what we long for, or He may do it by showing us what He can do when we submit our longings to His care.**

The love that Abraham felt for Ishmael was a **known quantity** to him – he knew and felt that love. He **could not understand** how much he would love all of his other children, just as we could not understand what life would be like once we had children.

Truth 4: UNDERSTANDING PRINCIPLE – A godly mother must believe that God touches the needs of all of your heart, when you trust Him with your whole heart (17:20). God deals with us in understanding of who we are and what we care about.

*Genesis 17:20 "As for Ishmael, I have heard you; behold, **I will bless him**, and will make him fruitful and will multiply him exceedingly. He shall become the father of twelve princes, and I will make him a great nation."*

God knows what we yearn for. If it is selfish – He will help us to see that. Yet, when we long for the good of others, God knows our heart. He will not simply say "Yes" to every request – that will not tell His story well. Yet, He will not ignore our heartfelt cry for others.

Abraham wanted Ishmael to experience the blessing of God – and God promised that he would. At the same time, Abraham couldn't feel for the others that he did not yet hold in his arms, but God could. Abraham needed to trust and know that God knew what he did not know.

What parent cannot understand the love he felt for little Ishmael?

Someone has astutely said that mothers measure things in different ways than others:

- Real mothers would like to be able to eat a whole candy bar (all by themselves) and drink a Coke without any "floaters" in it.
- Real mothers know that their kitchen utensils are probably going to end up in the sandbox.
- Real mothers know that dried play dough doesn't come out of shag carpets.
- Real mothers sometimes ask, "Why me?" and get the answer when a little voice says, "Because I love you best."
- Real mothers know that a child's growth is not measured by height or years or grade…It is marked by the progression of Mama to Mom to Mother…

Truth 5: PATH PRINCIPLE – A godly mother must recognize that God doesn't wait for US to make the plan – His blessing to us is revealing a bit of our part in it.

Genesis 17:21-22 "But My covenant I will establish with Isaac, whom Sarah will bear to you at this season next year." 22 When He finished talking with him, God went up from Abraham….

The fact is we have fewer plans to make than we have paths to follow. God has a story for us to tell. He knows how He wants the story to be told. The only problem is I don't know how He wants the story to be told in every case.

The **Path Principle** is this: When I follow what God has told me, God uncovers more of the path that is hidden beneath my feet. Following His path is following blessing. It simply requires that I believe what He has said and conform my life to the things He has promised -- even before I can see them happen.

Susannah Wesley, who bore 17 children, made time each week to take each of those boys and girls aside and counsel with them, speaking to them about the love of Jesus. Is it any wonder that one boy in that family became the greatest preacher of his generation, and another son became the greatest hymn writer in the English-speaking world?

With a mother like that, we can understand why Charles Wesley wrote these lines, ardent with devotion to Christ:

> "O for a thousand tongues to sing my great Redeemer's praise, the glories of my God and King, the triumphs of His grace! Jesus! The name that charms our fears, that bids our sorrows cease, 'tis music in the sinner's ears; 'tis life, and healthy, and peace."

Truth 6: SERVICE PRINCIPLE - A godly mother must believe that God's richest blessings are often opened to us inside a *package that appears to be WORK.*

Genesis 18:1-8: "The LORD appeared to him by the oaks of Mamre while he was sitting at the tent door in the heat of the day. 2 When he lifted up his eyes and looked, behold, three men were standing opposite him; and when he saw them, he ran from the tent door to meet them and bowed himself to the earth, 3 and said, "My Lord, if now I have found favor in your sight, please do not pass your servant by. 4 Please let a little water be brought and wash your feet, and rest yourselves under the tree; 5 and I will bring a piece of bread, that you may refresh yourselves; after that you may go on, since you have visited your servant." And they said, "So do, as you have said." 6 So

*Abraham hurried into the tent to Sarah, and said, "**Quickly**, prepare three measures of fine flour, knead it and make bread cakes." 7 Abraham also ran to the herd, and took a tender and choice calf and gave it to the servant, and he (the servant) hurried to prepare it. 8 He took curds and milk and the calf which he (Abraham) had [previously] prepared, and placed it before them; and he was standing by them under the tree as they ate."*

First, we must recognize the WORK involved in building a family that walks with God. Someone has said: "**The hand that rocks the cradle usually is attached to someone who isn't getting enough sleep**." (quoted from John Fiebig)

Note that Abraham and Sarah:

- OBSERVED POTENTIAL FOR SERVICE - saw an opportunity (18:1-2a).

- REFLECTED DESIRE - eagerly ran to meet a need (18:2b).

- DELIBERATELY RANKED - humbly served (18:2b).

- ADDED VALUE - sought ways to be more useful to the others (18:3-4).

- BUILT PATTERNS: Abraham and Sarah had a pattern of serving (outsiders and each other) built into their lives (18:6a) – that made his words to her less sharp, and her desire to fulfill the request ready.

- AGREED VALUES: The couple built a trust in his family over basic values and the use of resources (18:7a).

- PURPOSEFUL SAVINGS: The family built up resources (servants, livestock) for the purpose of blessing others (18:7b). The family saved beyond their daily use, and was able to become a blessing to others (18:8).

Truth 7: PATTERN PRINCIPLE – A godly mother recognizes that God can use even our weakness to build a pattern of blessing for generations to come (18:9-16). It is easy to get discouraged at our lives, our growth, and our defeats. God can and will use them all to tell His story!

Genesis 18:9 Then they said to him, "Where is Sarah your wife?" And he said, "There, in the tent." 10 He said, "I will surely return to you at this time next year; and behold, Sarah your wife will have a son." And Sarah was listening at the tent door, which was behind him. 11 Now Abraham and Sarah were old, advanced in age; Sarah was past childbearing. 12 Sarah laughed to herself, saying, "After I have become old, shall I have pleasure, my lord being old also?" 13 And the LORD said to Abraham, "Why did Sarah laugh, saying, 'Shall I indeed bear a child, when I am so old?' 14 Is anything too difficult for the LORD? At the appointed time I will return to you, at this time next year, and Sarah will have a son." 15 Sarah denied it however, saying, "I did not laugh," for she was afraid. And He said, "No, but you did laugh." 16 Then the men rose up from there, and looked down toward Sodom; and Abraham was walking with them to send them off.

"A little boy forgot his lines in a Sunday school presentation. His mother was in the front row to prompt him. She gestured and formed the words silently with her lips, but it did not help. Her son's memory was blank. Finally, she leaned forward and whispered the cue, "I am the light of the world." The child beamed and with great feeling and a loud clear voice said, "My mother is the light of the world." (*Bits and Pieces*, 1989)

We will become an example with our lives – either positive or negative. **God used the pattern of Sarah's life to help a poor Nazareth girl have confidence that Messiah would be born in her**. She could have laughed it off, but the pattern of blessing – God doing the impossible through the unlikely – was rooted in her heart from a story of old!

You do not know how your story will affect the ages of your children to come. Your obedience today may not have startling effects on the world --- yet. Don't underestimate the power of bringing glory to God from an ordinary, but surrendered life!

Mom, your surrender to God as a mom is vital to the blessing of your family, and the future of your heritage. God will bless you with glimpses of His glory for that surrender.

Reading the Map:
Lessons in Genesis

Lesson Eighteen: Genesis 18:16 - 19:3
"Choosing My Stage"

They want to live in the hottest town! They want to have it all and be connected to all the "happening" people. They want to blow the dust off of their feet from the small no-name places where they grew up and find themselves in the thick of it all. They want the excitement! Sadly, with the great launch forward, the choosing of a stage to live out their lives is not well thought through. One day they awaken to find themselves surrounded by people they do not choose to be like, and do not choose to be around.

Evil tolerated is like termites ignored. "No one smells good in a cesspool." So goes the old line. It is a reminder that evil easily contaminates, but good is hard to spread. Some believers grasp early on the need to choose carefully the stage where they live their lives -- but many do not.

Key Principle: Godliness isn't only about how I act; it is about where I choose to place myself.

It is about the kind of people we surround ourselves with and the contaminating things we learn to tolerate in our lives...

Both Abraham and Lot chose a place to live out their walk with God:

- **Abraham**: 18:1 Now the LORD appeared to him by the oaks of Mamre, while he was sitting at the tent door in the heat of the day.
- **Lot**: 19:1a Now the two angels came to Sodom in the evening as Lot was sitting in the gate of Sodom...

Lot was there because he **chose** to be there in spite of the reputation of the people. It was a place of relative luxury and comfort, and perhaps he thought he could reason with the people there. The only clue we have to his reasons are found in the passage that tells of his selection of the place.

Genesis 13:10 Lot lifted up his eyes and saw all the valley of the Jordan, that it was well watered everywhere—this was before the LORD destroyed Sodom and Gomorrah—like the garden of the LORD, like the land of Egypt as you go to Zoar. 11 So Lot chose for himself all the valley of the Jordan, and Lot journeyed eastward. Thus they separated from each other. 12 Abram settled in the land of Canaan, while Lot settled in the cities of the valley, and moved his tents as far as Sodom. 13 Now the men of Sodom were wicked exceedingly and sinners against the LORD.

- The place where Abraham settled was west of Hebron in an area outside of the city. It was a setting surrounded by vineyards and pathways for shepherds and sheep.
- The place where Lot settled was a well-watered plain that appeared to offer creature comforts.

At the time of Lot's choice, God already inserted into the narrative the notion that the men of Sodom were very wicked. We cannot tell if this is intended simply to be retrospective, or if it implies that Lot knew of their wickedness.

The central point of the narrative is this: both of these men had the option to choose places to live out their faith.

Many of us have a similar choice -- choosing to live near friends or family, or far away because of job opportunities.

Lot was not wrong because he chose an easy place, nor was he wrong for choosing a place away from his family. He wasn't even wrong for choosing a place that was evil. **The wrong part of his choice was remaining there when it was clear that that environment would not produce lives that were pleasing to God.**

We are not responsible to know what a situation will be like before we get into it (unless there are indications that it is unwise or dangerous), but we are expected to move on when we find the environment we are in drags our families down. Mature believers stand up for the values of their family, and look out for the future by placing themselves and their families in a place where they can flourish in godliness. Particularly among believers, some of us have brought into our homes people who have negatively impacted our children and reflected values that were ungodly and because we thought we could change them.

We need to be very careful about the environment are children are brought up in. For that matter, we need to be careful about the environment we allow ourselves to remain in.

They both reflected some solid positive values:

- Abraham saw an opportunity to minister and worked at it:

*Genesis 18:2-7 When he lifted up his eyes and looked, behold, three men were standing opposite him; and when he saw them, he **ran** from the tent door to meet them and **bowed** himself to the earth, 3 and said, "My Lord, if now I have found favor in Your sight, **please do not pass** Your servant by. 4 Please let a little water be brought and wash your feet, and rest yourselves under the tree; 5 and I will bring a piece of bread that you may refresh yourselves; after that you may go on, since you have visited your servant." And they said, "So do, as you have said."*

- Lot saw an opportunity to minister and worked at it:

*Genesis 19:1 Now the two angels came to Sodom in the evening as Lot was sitting in the gate of Sodom. When Lot saw them, he rose to meet them and **bowed** down with his face to the ground. 2 And he said, "Now behold, my lords, **please turn aside into your servant's house**, and spend the night, and wash your feet; then you may rise early and go on your way." They said however, "No, but we shall spend the night in the square." 3 Yet **he urged them strongly**, so they turned aside to him and entered his house; and he prepared a feast for them, and baked unleavened bread, and they ate.*

As we have seen from earlier studies in the *Bible*, clearly a walk with God is reflected in choices. One of the ways to see through a façade and into the true character of a person is to place that person in any position of discomfort or pressure.

In the ancient society of the near East, one of the great expectations that placed pressure on people of importance was hospitality. A man was measured by the meal he placed in front of others, and the comfort he offered them. Both Abraham and Lot had a chance to host the messengers of God. When you look carefully at the narrative, you discover that both of them shared strong values in this area.

In a sense, we could say that both of these men were good men. They both wanted to do right. They both saw opportunities to serve, and they acted on them. From all that we can see in the story, both acted as God would have them. There is but a slight difference between the two. Abraham offers hospitality out of his desire to serve while Lot offers hospitality with the urgency that the men must not stay elsewhere. The fact that he urged them strongly tips the story toward us, showing that Lot understood the perils of the place he had chosen to live and bring up his children. Without this detail, we would have concluded that Lot must have been somehow disconnected from the reality of those he lived among -- though he sat at a place of the judges of the city (and it is rather hard to believe that he did not know their character).

Even godly people make ungodly decisions. Even more mature believers sometimes fall into compromise and cannot see the danger that lies ahead. When they become aware of the danger, they dilute themselves into believing, "I can handle this!"

The question is not whether they can, the question is whether **God intends them to. They both surrounded themselves with people that showed their character when pressed:**

- **Abraham**: *Genesis 18:6 So **Abraham** hurried into the tent to **Sarah**, and said, "Quickly, prepare three measures of fine flour, knead it and make bread cakes." 7 Abraham also ran to the herd, and took a tender and choice calf and gave it to the **servant**, and he hurried to prepare it. 8 He took curds and milk* *and the calf which he had prepared, and placed it before them; and he was standing by them under the tree as they ate.*

- **Lot**: *Genesis 19:4 Before they lay down, the men of the city, the **men of Sodom**, surrounded the house, both **young** and **old**, all the people from every quarter; 5 and they called to Lot and said to him, "Where are the men who came to you tonight? Bring them out to us that we may have relations with them." 6 But Lot went out to them at the doorway, and shut the door behind him, 7 and said, "**Please, my brothers, do not act wickedly**. 8 Now behold, I have two daughters who have not had relations with man; please let me bring them out to you, and do to them whatever you like; only do nothing to these men, inasmuch as they have come under the shelter of my roof." 9 But they said, "Stand aside." Furthermore, they said, "**This one came in as an alien, and already he is acting like a judge; now we will treat you worse than them**." So they pressed hard against Lot and came near to break the door. 10 But the men reached out their hands and brought Lot into the house with them, and shut the door. 11 They struck the men who were at the doorway of the house with blindness, both small and great, so that they wearied themselves trying to find the doorway.*

One of the obvious differences between Abraham and Lot can be seen in their choice of companions. Abraham surrounded himself with workers that were chosen to accomplish tasks that would help support the family. He lived a simple life with his wife Sarah, though he lived in comparative luxury as a wealthy member of society. It is clear in the *Bible* that the bulk of his life he spent in a tent, but we should not mistake this for a rugged existence -- by comparison to his fellows. We do see that Abraham chose a place away from the cities of his day. Obviously, he made his living as a shepherd. Yet, there were wide open spaces between villages in the Hebron plateau. In other words, he could have lived in a city but chose to raise his family in a way slightly more isolated than the norm. He knew he was not of this people, and though he lived among them, he kept some distance.

Lot chose to be in the city, and sat at the heart of the decision-making part of the city. He sat where the judges sat -- in the gate. He surrounded himself with men whose character yielded awful acts, and he tried to reason with them. Abraham found that it was not profitable to try and argue with evil men to live righteously. Lot on the other hand, was a bit of an optimist – **he thought he could talk evil men into good decisions**. Not only that, **Lot misunderstood his relationship with the people around him**. **He thought they saw him as one of them**. When push came to shove, they saw him as an outsider trying to push his morality on them.

How many young believers make this mistake! Because the world is all on your side when you offer them something, they fail to see **that the relationship will be short-lived when they take a moral stand**.

They both saw their wives hesitant to truly follow God:

- Abraham: **Sarah** laughed at the idea that God was going to give her a future as a mom! *Genesis 8:9 Then they said to him, "Where is Sarah your wife?" And he said, "There, in the tent." 10 He said, "I will surely return to you at this time next year; and behold, Sarah your **wife** will have a son." And Sarah was listening at the tent door, which was behind him. 11 Now Abraham and Sarah were old, advanced in age; Sarah was past childbearing. 12 Sarah laughed to herself, saying, "After I have become old, shall I have pleasure, my lord being old also?" 13 And the LORD said to Abraham, "Why did Sarah laugh, saying, 'Shall I indeed bear a child, when I am so old?' 14 Is anything too difficult for the LORD? At the appointed time I will return to you, at this time next year, and Sarah will have a son." 15 Sarah denied it however, saying, "I did not laugh"; for she was afraid. And He said, "No, but you **did** laugh."* **Remember, we noted that this unbelief mirrored Abraham's own in Genesis 17:16** *[The LORD said:] "I will bless her, and indeed I will give you a son by her. Then I will bless her, and she shall be a mother of nations; kings of peoples will come from her." 17Then Abraham fell on his face and laughed, and said in his heart, "Will a child be born to a man one hundred years old? And will Sarah, who is ninety years old, bear a child?"*

- Lot: **His wife** also scoffed at God's call to the future...*Genesis 19:12 Then the two men said to Lot, "Whom else have you here? A **son-in-law**, and your **sons**, and your* *daughters (virgins as mentioned in 19:8 when Lot said, "I have two daughters who have not had relations with man"), and whomever you have in the city, bring them out of the place; 13 for we are about to destroy this place, because their outcry has become so great before the LORD that the LORD has sent us to destroy it." 14 Lot went out and **spoke to his sons-in-law**, who **were to marry his daughters,** and said, "Up, get out of this place, for the LORD will destroy the city." But he appeared to his sons-in-law to be **jesting**. 15 When morning dawned, the angels urged Lot, saying, "Up, take your wife and your two daughters who are here, or you will be swept away in the punishment of the city." 16 But he **hesitated**. So the men **seized** his hand and the hand of his **wife** and the hands of his two **daughters**, for the compassion of the LORD was upon him; and they brought him out, and put him outside the city. 17 When they had brought them outside, one said, "Escape for your life! **Do not look behind you**, and do not stay anywhere in the valley; escape to the mountains, or you will be swept away." ....24 Then the LORD rained on Sodom and Gomorrah brimstone and fire from the LORD out of Heaven, 25 and He overthrew those cities, and all the valley, and all the inhabitants of the cities, and what grew on the ground. 26 But his **wife**, from behind him, looked back, and she became a pillar of salt.*

Both Abraham and Lot married women who found it difficult to trust God for their future. In the case of Sarah, the revealed truth of God was that she would bear a child. Her age advanced well past menopause led her to believe this would not be the case. In the case of Lot's wife, we know only that she was unwilling to see her future with an attitude of complete trust.

The point is that even mature believers should anticipate the people around them struggling. We are impacted by the people we spend our time with.

In Sarah's case, **she spent her time with a doubting husband** -- so she doubted as well. In the case of Lot's wife, **she surrounded herself with the goods of this world**, and could not see the good of watching them destroyed by her Master. She could not find it in her heart to simply obey God, no matter how powerfully He demonstrated Himself.

They both experienced God's Word in grace:

- **Abraham interceded for those among the evil men (his family)**:

*Genesis 18:16 Then the men rose up from there, and looked down toward Sodom; and Abraham was walking with them to send them off. 17 The LORD said, "Shall I hide from Abraham what I am about to do, 18 since Abraham will surely become a great and mighty nation, and in him all the nations of the Earth will be blessed? 19 For I have chosen him, so that he may command his children and his household after him to keep the way of the LORD by doing righteousness and justice, so that the LORD may bring upon Abraham what He has spoken about him." 20 And the LORD said, **"The outcry of Sodom and Gomorrah is indeed great, and their sin is exceedingly grave. 21 I will go down now, and see if they have done entirely according to its outcry, which has come to Me; and if not, I will know."** 22 Then the men turned away from there and went toward Sodom, while Abraham was still standing before the LORD. 23 Abraham came near and said, "Will You indeed sweep away the righteous with the wicked? 24 Suppose there are **fifty** righteous within the city; will You indeed sweep it away and not spare the place for the sake of the fifty righteous who are in it? 25 Far be it from You to do such a thing, to slay the righteous with the wicked, so that the righteous and the wicked are treated alike. Far be it from You! Shall not the Judge of all the earth deal justly?" 26 So the LORD said, "If I find in Sodom fifty righteous within the city, then I will spare the whole place on their account." 27 And Abraham replied, "Now behold, I have ventured to speak to the Lord, although I am but dust and ashes. 28 Suppose the fifty righteous are lacking five, will You destroy the whole city because of five?" And He said, "I will not destroy it if I find **forty-five** there." 29 He spoke to Him yet again and said, "Suppose forty are found there?" And He said, "I will not do it on account of the **forty**." 30 Then he said, "Oh may the Lord not be angry, and I shall speak; suppose **thirty** are found there?" And He said, "I will not do it if I find thirty there." 31 And he said, "Now behold, I have ventured to speak to the Lord; suppose **twenty** are found there?" And He said, "I will not destroy it on account of the twenty." 32 Then he said, "Oh may the Lord not be angry, and I shall speak only this once; suppose* *ten* are found there?" And He said, "I will not destroy it on account of the ten."

- **Lot tried to reason with those who were saving him**:

Genesis 19:17 When they had brought them outside, one said, "Escape for your life! **Do not look behind you**, *and do not stay anywhere in the valley; escape to the mountains, or you will be swept away." 18 But Lot said to them, "Oh no, my lords! 19 Now behold, your servant has found favor in your sight, and you have magnified your lovingkindness, which you have shown me by saving my life;* **but I cannot escape to the mountains**, *for the* **disaster will overtake me** *and I will die; 20 now behold, this town is near enough to flee to, and it is small. Please, let me escape there (is it not small?) that my life may be saved." 21 He said to him, "Behold, I grant you this request also, not to overthrow the town of which you have spoken. 22* **"Hurry, escape there, for I cannot do anything until you arrive there**." *Therefore the name of the town was called Zoar. 23 The sun had risen over the Earth when Lot came to Zoar. 24 Then the LORD rained on Sodom and Gomorrah brimstone and fire from the LORD out of Heaven, 25 and He overthrew those cities, and all the valley, and all the inhabitants of the cities, and what grew on the ground. 26 But his wife, from behind him, looked back, and she became a pillar of salt.*

One of the great benefits of following God is the exposure to truth we could not know if He did not tell us. The fact is, **God's Word becomes important only to those who believe it and obey it**.

- In the case of Abraham, God shared His plan to investigate Sodom -- and this gave Abraham a chance to intercede on behalf of his family.
- In the case of Lot, he found himself interceding on his own behalf -- not on behalf of others. This happened because he placed himself in such peril through his choices that he was in need of assistance, and not in a place where he could offer assistance.

Believers need to make choices about the kind of places they will live and people they will live among that include ways to grow themselves to the point where they can build up others. They are not simply in it for themselves -- they are looking for ways they can bless others. **When our choices are made poorly, our ability to bless others is hampered**. Often instead of becoming a blessing, we **find ourselves in need of others to bless us**. Lot found that out.

They both saw where their choices led them:

- Abraham:

*Genesis 18:33 As soon as He had finished speaking to Abraham the LORD departed, and Abraham **returned to his place**.... 19:27 Now Abraham arose early in the morning and went to the place where he had stood before the LORD; 28 and he looked down toward Sodom and Gomorrah, and toward all the land of the valley, and he saw, and behold, the smoke of the land ascended like the smoke of a furnace. 29 Thus it came about, when God destroyed the cities of the valley, that **God remembered Abraham, and sent Lot out** of the midst of the overthrow, when He overthrew the cities in which Lot lived.*

- Lot:

Genesis 19:27 Now Abraham arose early in the morning and went to the place where he had stood before the LORD; 28 and he looked down toward Sodom and Gomorrah, and toward all the land of the valley, and he saw, and behold, the smoke of the land ascended like the smoke of a furnace. 29 Thus it came about, when God destroyed the   cities of the valley, that God remembered Abraham, and sent Lot out of the midst of the overthrow, when He overthrew the cities in which Lot lived. 30 Lot went up from Zoar and stayed in the mountains, and his two daughters with him; for he was afraid to stay in Zoar; and he stayed in a cave, he and his two daughters. 31 Then the firstborn said to the younger, "Our father is old, and there is not a man on Earth to come in to us after the manner of the Earth. 32 Come, let us make our father drink wine, and let us lie with him that we may preserve our family through our father." 33 So they made their father drink wine that night, and the firstborn went in and lay with her father; and he did not know when she lay down or when she arose. 34 On the following day, the firstborn said to the younger, "Behold, I lay last night with my father; let us make him drink wine tonight also; then you go in and lie with him, that we may preserve our family through our father." 35 So they made their father drink wine that night also, and the younger arose and lay with him; and he did not know when she lay down or when she arose. 36 Thus both the daughters of Lot were with child by their father. 37 The firstborn bore a son, and called his name Moab; he is the father of the Moabites to this day. 38 As for the younger, she also bore a son, and called his name Ben-ammi; he is the father of the sons of Ammon to this day.

Lot thought he could raise his children surrounded by evil, walk amidst evil, and reason with it. In the end, he lost his home, his wife, his daughters' honorable future and was left in a cave with the values the daughters learned permeating the atmosphere. He drank and slept – because it hurt too much to live. It wasn't that he personally wasn't a good man – it is that he chose a stage for his life that left him with nothing.

- **They both chose a place to live out their walk with God.**

- **They both chose to personally reflect some solid positive values.**

- **They both chose to surrounded themselves with people that showed their character when pressed.**

- **They both saw their wives hesitant to truly follow God.**

- **They both experienced God's Word in grace.**

- **They both saw where their choices led them. One was remembered and blessed (with some of that blessing falling on his family) and the other was left in a cave with daughters who reflected the evil of the world they were raised in.**

Solomon warned the children of Israel much later that the difficult days of life will soon come and **only those who prepare**

with a walk with God will face them well (Eccl. 12:1b) -
because our minds will eventually fade – our "brightness" slip,
as well as our bodies ability to recoup quickly.

*Eccl. 12:2 Remember also your Creator in the days of your
youth, before the evil days come and the years draw near when
you will say, "I have no delight in them;" 2 before the sun and
the light, the moon and the stars are darkened, and clouds
return after the rain.*

Many aspects of our path are chosen early in life. If we choose
well, we will live to see the fruit of that choice. If we choose
badly, thinking we will choose better later, we will slip through
life faster than we anticipate!

Continue with Solomon's words in Ecclesiastes 12:

- Growing weaker too soon, our hands tremble, our bodies
  are stooping, our teeth are coming out and our eyesight
  failing, as in 12:3 *in the day that the watchmen of the
  house tremble, and mighty men stoop, the grinding ones
  stand idle because they are few, and those who look
  through windows grow dim.*

- "Gumming" our food when the teeth fail (12:4a), failure to
  sleep well (12:4b) and failed hearing, as in 12:4b. *"and
  the doors on the street are shut as the sound of the
  grinding mill is low, and one will arise at the sound of the
  bird, and all the daughters of song will sing softly.*

- Fears of difficult physical challenges become very real
  (12:5) as our hair turns white. Limbs will grow stiff and
  sexual drives will fail (*'abiyownah: ab-ee-yo-naw'* – a
  stimulating taste), as a man yields this life and passes to
  eternity - and is remembered... as in 12:5b.
  *"Furthermore, men are afraid of a high place and of
  terrors on the road; the almond tree blossoms, the
  grasshopper drags himself along, and the caperberry is
  ineffective. For man goes to his eternal home while
  mourners go about in the street."*

- The spinal column weakens, the mind becomes dulled and the bowels become unpredictable, in addition to the accompanying heart problems. As in 12:6. *"Remember Him before the silver cord is broken and the golden bowl is crushed, the pitcher by the well is shattered and the wheel at the cistern is crushed."*

- In the end, the body is laid to rest and turns back to dust and memories, while the spirit is whisked into eternity.. as in 12:7. *Then the dust will return to the earth as it was, and the spirit will return to God Who gave it.*

- It all passes quickly, and much *that appears to have meaning*, really doesn't! See how Solomon closed the passage? *12:8. "Vanity of vanities," says the Preacher, "all is vanity!*

The choice is not just **WHAT** we do, but **WHERE** we choose to live our lives, and **WHO** we choose to surround ourselves with as we live them. **Godliness isn't only about how we act, it is about where we choose to place ourselves - the kind of people we surround ourselves with and the contaminating things we learn to tolerate in our lives.** Lot found out the hard way that the days slip away too fast, and **evil tolerated is like termites ignored.**

"Dr. Ralph Sockman writes about an experience he had while standing on the edge of Niagara Falls one clear, cold March day. Wrapped in white winter garments, the falls glistened in the bright sun. As some birds swooped down to snatch a drink from the clear water, Sockman's companion told how he had seen birds carried over the edge of the precipice. As they dipped down for a drink, tiny droplets of ice would form on their wings. As they returned for additional drinks more ice would weigh down their bodies until they couldn't rise above the cascading waters. Flapping their wings, the birds would suddenly drop over the falls." (*Today in the Word*, October, 1990, p. 14.)

A man purchased a white mouse to use as food for his pet snake. He dropped the unsuspecting mouse into the snake's glass cage, where the snake was sleeping in a bed of sawdust. The tiny mouse had a serious problem on his hands. At any moment he could be swallowed alive. Obviously, the mouse needed to come up with a brilliant plan. What did the terrified creature do?

He quickly set up work covering the snake with sawdust chips until it was completely buried. With that, the mouse apparently thought he had solved his problem. The solution, however, came from outside. The man took pity on the silly little mouse and removed him from the cage. No matter how hard we try to cover or deny our sinful nature, it's fool's work. **Sin will eventually awake from sleep and shake off its cover. Were it not for the saving grace of the Master's hand, sin would eat us alive.**

Reading the Map:
Lessons in Genesis

Lesson Nineteen: Genesis 20
"Connecting the Dots"

Did you ever feel like life was running so fast that you weren't sure which traffic lane you were supposed to be in? A young student once said: "Knowing my life, when my ship comes in, I will be standing at Gate 27 of the airport half a city away!" We live fast-paced lives with many connections playing out at the same time. Is it possible in our ever-connected "Facebook world," we may have failed to make the one connection that makes all the others work?

We don't always connect the right things, but we often DO connect the wrong ones. We jump to conclusions. Even worse, we live in **embarrassment** and connect ourselves wrongly to the actions of someone else that we were not called to be responsible for.

Our story today is about a **missed connection** and a **wrong connection**. Abraham **wrongly connected to embarrassment** of a family scandal created by Lot (his nephew) and Lot's daughters. That mistake caused him to make uncharacteristic choices – wrong choices – to withdraw from his place of testimony at Mamre, to endanger his wife's purity, and to deceive the Prince of Gerar.

Those choices were wrong – but they were not the root problem, they were symptoms of a bigger problem. **Abraham placed the call of God and God's revealed truths concerning His life direction** beneath the circumstances. He missed the connection between his choices from God's truth purposes in his life as revealed in God's Word.

As a believer, we must understand the deeper truth of this passage, because the symptoms change, but the disease shows itself often.

Key Principle: I need to connect the daily choices I make to the purposes God has set forth in His Word for me – or my faith is just a series of platitudes.

We need to connect God's revealed Word to our choices. Many small choice "course corrections" can keep us in the right path. We must not look for the DRAMATIC choices as the normal path – but make the small, daily walk choices that honor the King.

Consider Three Important Truths

Truth One: We fail to connect God to our daily choices when we accept responsibility for what is NOT OURS.

*Genesis 20:1 **Now** Abraham journeyed from there toward the land of the Negev, and settled between Kadesh and Shur; then he sojourned in Gerar.*

The passage opens with **"NOW ABRAHAM JOURNEYED"**...Wait a minute! Didn't he have a great life at Mamre? What got him out of his tent? Oh, that's right, it was the story of Lot that caused Abraham to move. Did the Canaanites of the land know about his nephew? Why YES, since Abraham made a grand play to save him by raising a private army some years back. But then Lot made choices that Abraham hoped were not as bad as they appeared to be. He argued with the angels in hopes that the family of his nephew was still walking in righteousness. No, the word was out that Lot was saved, but Sodom was lost. More than that, Lot's daughters were with child by sleeping with their father, and the family's choices were a disgrace.

The Timing Reveals Abraham's Wrong Connection – accepting improper responsibility:

Matthew Henry long ago noted: "We are not told upon what occasion he removed, whether terrified by the destruction of Sodom, or because the country round was for the present prejudiced by it, or, as some of the Jewish writers say, because he was grieved at Lot's incest with his daughters, and the reproach which the Canaanites cast upon him and his religion, for his kinsman's sake: doubtless there was some good cause for his removal." (Matthew Henry Commentary on Genesis).

Abraham was **embarrassed** by Lot, and felt the need to **move his family to a remote place**. He was perhaps **getting questions about his own marriage**, and the way the Hebrews practiced their family life...**He appears to be making decisions out of embarrassment and shame, connecting his choices more to the circumstances** than to the call of God in his life.

This is how the Webster's Dictionary defines these two words:

- **EMBAR'RASSED**, pp. Perplexed; rendered intricate; confused; confounded.
- **SHAME**, n. A painful sensation excited by a consciousness of guilt, or of having done something which injures reputation; or by of that which nature or modesty prompts us to conceal. Shame is particularly excited by the disclosure of actions which, in the view of men, are mean and degrading. Hence it is often or always manifested by a downcast look or by blushes, called confusion of face.

The Places <u>Reveal Abraham's Wrong Connection</u> to Lot's sins:

- Between *Kadesh* and *Shur* means the edge of livable space – the "get away from everyone" solution for a time. This was a temporary move, followed by a second move much further north to the area of Gerar. In the *modus operandi* of Abraham, a **MOVE is often the beginning of a series of bad choices, when the move is not directed by God**. Abraham was in the grip of God's blessings when he decided to move to the Negev (see Genesis 12) and ended up in Egypt because of a famine.

- It was after that that Abraham journeyed – probably needing supplies, to the western Negev Basin, ostensibly out of the reach of the reputation of the Canaanites of the Mamre region of the Hebron Plateau.

The "Strategy of Deception" <u>Unveils Abraham's Wrong Connection</u> – to embarrassment and away from his call.

Genesis 20:2 Abraham said of Sarah his wife, "She is my sister." So Abimelech king of Gerar sent and took Sarah.

Back to the same play Abraham used in Egypt years before, that caused him so many problems.

Why pull that play out again? Because Abraham had chosen years before to include that in his "play book" on life. In 20:13, Abraham revealed to the prince that this was a play he planned to use periodically if things weren't going well and the situation warranted it. Integrity is a root trait of our lives, as is a flawed view of it.

We can change the idea of wrong into right in our own minds when we twist integrity within.

The issue before (Genesis 12) was Abraham's **fear** concerning Sarah's beauty. This was **MANY**
years later, and no longer the issue. Note the earlier event:

Genesis 12:10 Now there was a famine in the land; so Abram went down to Egypt to sojourn there, for the famine was severe in the land. 11 It came about when he came near to Egypt, that he said to Sarai his wife, "See now, I know that you are a beautiful woman; 12 and when the Egyptians see you, they will say, 'This is his wife'; and they will kill me, but they will let you live. 13 Please say that you are my sister so that it may go well with me because of you, and that I may live on account of you." 14 It came about when Abram came into Egypt, the Egyptians saw that the woman was very beautiful. 15 Pharaoh's officials saw her and praised her to Pharaoh; and the woman was taken into Pharaoh's house. 16 Therefore he treated Abram well for her sake; and gave him sheep and oxen and donkeys and male and female servants and female donkeys and camels. 17 But the LORD struck Pharaoh and his house with great plagues because of Sarai, Abram's wife.

When Abraham feared, a plan to deceive that he reckoned in his own mind was justified and popped out. Here it came again in Genesis 20.

Stop here for a second and consider the deeper truth here...

John Robb, Unreached Peoples Program Director with World Vision says: "Satan works... by trapping a people in society-wide presumptions about reality. In settings where Christ is not obeyed... such strongholds go unchallenged, sometimes for centuries, gaining strength with every passing generation." (*Perspectives*, 145-151)

This process in our society began when believers stopped learning God's Word well, and substituted the world's ideas for the Word's truths. As time went on, we lost our voices in the public sector because we weren't saying something distinct.

If Lot's incest was an issue, perhaps the "half-sister" issue of Abraham became an embarrassment to him. Ironically, he may have moved because he was taking harassment for Lot's actions, and maybe even a misunderstanding of his own.

Abraham concluded that Lot's daughters and Sarah's status made him vulnerable in the Canaanite culture no matter where he was – choosing to keep their marriage arrangement a secret, rather than explaining the God-ordained arrangement of his life.

Abraham later had occasion to comfortably explain his actions when he knew that his life was no longer threatened.

*Genesis 20:11 Abraham said, "**Because I thought, surely there is no fear of God in this place, and they will kill me because of my wife**. 12 Besides, she actually is my sister, the daughter of my father, but not the daughter of my mother, and she became my wife; 13 and it came about, when God caused me to wander from my father's house, that I said to her, 'This is the kindness which you will show to me: everywhere we go, say of me, "He is my brother."'"*

Truth Two: When we fail to connect God to our daily choices it is the revelation of God's Word that can push us back in line!

*Genesis 20:3 But **God came to Abimelech** in a dream of the night, and said to him, "Behold, you are a dead man because of the woman whom you have taken, for she is married." 4 Now Abimelech had not come near her; and he said, "Lord, will You slay a nation, even though blameless? 5 "Did he not himself say to me, 'She is my sister'? And she herself said, 'He is my brother.' In the integrity of my heart and the innocence of my hands I have done this." 6 Then God said to him in the dream, "Yes, I know that in the integrity of your heart you have done this, and I also kept you from sinning against Me; therefore I did not let you touch her. 7 Now therefore, restore the man's wife, for he is a prophet, and he will pray for you and you will live. But if you do not restore her, know that you shall surely die, you and all who are yours."*

God's Intervention moved Abraham back to obedience and protected his call.

God intervened three times in the narrative – though it is not obvious by the way the story was told.

FIRST INTERVENTION: The acquisition of Sarah (held in purity so as to leave the heritage of Isaac unquestioned) **was followed by a terrible problem of "womb closing" in Gerar**.

We have few details, but we know this from the end of the chapter: *Genesis 20:17 Abraham prayed to God, and God healed Abimelech and his wife and his maids, so that they bore children. 18 For the LORD had **closed fast all the wombs** of the household of Abimelech because of Sarah, Abraham's wife.'*

Because of the shortness of the time between their arrival and the apparent malady, we are left to wonder how they knew the wombs were closed. The term "close fast" is "aw-tsar': to restrain, retain, confine, restrict. The Hebrew term for womb is *rechem* a term with a "bonding and compassion root linked to the word for compassionate or *rachaman*.

When we call God Ha-Rachaman in Hebrew prayers - "The Compassionate One," we're connecting Him to the bond He created in the woman's womb. The root refers to *the deep love bond* (such as childbirth).

God shows the one who fears Him this same sort of compassion: Like as a father pities his children, so the LORD pities (*richam*) them that fear him (Psalm 103:13).

The point is probably that the monthly cycles of the maidens were interrupted, or more poignantly, they may have had ill-timed bleeding – keeping all of the city on edge of something unusual from the outset.

Abimelech may have gone to bed that night worrying about the meaning of what he was hearing about.

SECOND INTERVENTION: There was evidently some attempt to consummate a sexual union that was interrupted in a way that Abimelech and God both knew and understood.

God says that He "kept Abimelech from sinning" (20:6b), implying that something interrupted Abimelech's plan. It could be that Abimelech intended to sleep with her, but with the impending blood crisis, he assumed he could not.

THIRD INTERVENTION: This is marked by the dream mentioned in the passage from 20:3-7, where God made *Abimelech aware of the entire situation and its causes.*

*Genesis 20:8-13 So Abimelech arose early in the morning and called all his servants and told all these things in their hearing; and the men were greatly frightened. 9 Then Abimelech called Abraham and said to him, "**What have you done to us**? And how have I sinned against you, that you have brought on me and on my kingdom a great sin? You have done to me things **that ought not to be done**." 10 And Abimelech said to Abraham, "What have you encountered, that you have done this thing?" 11 Abraham said, "**Because I thought, surely there is no fear of God in this place, and they will kill me because of my wife**. 12 Besides, she actually is my sister, the daughter of* *my father, but not the daughter of my mother, and she became my wife; 13 and it came about, when God caused me to wander from my father's house, that I said to her, 'This is the kindness which you will show to me: everywhere we go, say of me, "He is my brother."'*

Abraham's Explanation reveals his flawed choices - he ignored connection with God in his choice:

Abraham tried to explain his rationale in the face of a lost reputation (the very thing he was running from to preserve?):

- I thought you would **not understand what God told** me to do in marrying my half- sister.
- I thought that **you would kill me** because you thought I was incestuous.
- In the face of God's intervention, let me explain that **I wasn't totally dishonest with you** – she is my half-sister, and I took it as an advantage and told Sarah long ago that this might be God's escape valve for us if it came up.

Truth Three: Even when we fail to connect God to our daily choices – He is not finished with us YET!

Pastor Mark Bruner wrote: Is there anyone who hasn't felt the sting of regret and discovered just how bitter it is to live with the thought that if only we hadn't done this or said that we'd be a whole lot happier at the moment? Beginning again is one "power" I wish that I had above all things in this life. I guess it is because I do a lot of things that I regret doing. Unfortunately, the doing and the regret are connected over time, with doing on one far end and regret on the other. **If only we could link these two things more closely; if only each of us had the power to start over when the end did not suit our intentions.**

"On New Year's Day, 1929, *Georgia Tech* played the *University of California* in the Rose Bowl. In that game a man named Roy Riegels recovered a fumble for California. Somehow, he became confused and started running 65 yards in the wrong direction.

That strange play came in the first half, and everyone who was watching the game was asking the same question: "What will Coach Nibbs Price do with Roy Riegels in the second half?" At half time Coach Price looked at the team and said simply, "Men the same team that played the first half will start the second." The players got up and started out, all but Riegels. The coach looked back and called to him; still he didn't move. Coach Price went over to where Riegels sat and said, "Roy, didn't you hear me? Then Roy Riegels looked up, his cheeks wet with a strong man's tears, and said. "Coach, I couldn't face that crowd in the stadium to save my life." Then Coach Price reached out and put his hand on Riegel's shoulder and said to him: "Roy, get up and go on back; the game is only half over." And Roy Riegels went back, and those Tech men will tell you that they have never seen a man play football as Roy Riegels played in that second half." (Haddon W .Robinson, *Christian Medical Society Journal*)

The *Bible* teaches us that what is done is done. There is no use in going back and reliving it or redoing it. God has one direction in life for us and that is forward, not backward. When King David sinned and displeased the Lord, God punished him for that sin and he grieved over it. Then, recognizing that the grief would not undo what he had undone, David put away his grief and "got back in the game."

Therein lies a valuable lesson for you and me. There is no way of going back, only going forward. When we sin, it is good to realize that the game is not over, only half over.

Genesis 20:14 Abimelech then took sheep and oxen and male and female servants, and gave them to Abraham, and restored his wife Sarah to him. 15 Abimelech said, "Behold, my land is before you; settle wherever you please." 16 To Sarah he said, "Behold, I have given your brother a thousand pieces of silver; behold, it is your vindication before all who are with you, and before all men you are cleared." 17 Abraham prayed to God, and God healed Abimelech and his wife and his maids, so that they bore children. 18 For the LORD had closed fast all the wombs of the household of Abimelech because of Sarah, Abraham's wife.

Outcomes:

- Abraham got a choice of land to live in (20:15),
- He acquired a thousand pieces of silver (20:16)
- He secured a clean bill of health for Sarah (20:16).
- Abraham prayed to the Lord and the curse of the womb was lifted (20:17).

Commentators and Christian teachers focus on what they see as Abraham's lie in the passage and get frustrated that it appears that Abraham does wrong and gets blessed. They miss the point.

Take, for instance, what the lesson commentator Matthew Henry offered in his comments on Genesis: "He had *been guilty of this same sin before,* and had been reproved for it, and convinced of the folly of the suggestion which induced him to it; yet he returns to it. Note: It is possible that a good man may, not only fall into sin, but relapse into the same sin, through the surprise and strength of temptation and the infirmity of the flesh. Let backsliders repent then, but not despair, Jer. 3:22."

He was under no obligation to explain the family relationship fully by any standard of God – **that wasn't the sin of the passage**.

The sin of the passage was that Abraham lost track of what God told him was his purpose in serving His Lord.

Abraham didn't connect the Word of God and His promises to his daily behavior – he lacked a connection of the dots. He was to experience the realization of God's undeserved grace and blessing in very specific ways:

- Bring blessing to the nations that blessed him (12:1).
- Become the physical father (15:4) of a great nation (12:2) with innumerable descendants (13:16), through Sarah his wife (17:19).
- Become the father of a multitude of other nations (17:5-6).

- Acquire a land for his children (12:7) as an everlasting inheritance and possession (17:8).

In order for those things to happen, Abraham had to protect Sarah from anything that would block that promise from taking shape. Lot's family embarrassed Abraham, and he thought he could better protect himself by withdrawing from his neighbors. The problem came when he was willing to trade Sarah's purity for his protection – and in the process lose the clear path to the blessing that comes when we take God seriously and at His Word.

Abraham felt he needed to protect himself from misunderstanding and embarrassment, and God stepped in to accomplish the greater protection of the passage – seeing to it that His holy purposes were accomplished. **He needed to connect the daily choices he made to the purposes God set forth in His Word for him.**

Reading the Map: Lessons in Genesis

Reading the Map:
Lessons in Genesis

Lesson Twenty: Genesis 21:1-2
"Encore for a Villain"

The hero and the villain fought viciously until, at last, the villain stopped his fight, and slunk down as though dead. The hero stood up, his face beaming because he had overcome evil. His eyes met the damsel he rescued from her distress. As his lips gave way to smile, the eyes of the maiden widened, for the villain was not dead, but standing behind our hero, ready to pounce upon him with a deadly weapon.

The shot fired, and you are left in the pause wondering, "Who fired the shot? Who was hit by the bullet?" And finally, the villain slumps to the ground. Pan up the camera, and the damsel that was moments ago being rescued became the rescuer.

How many times have you seen this "premature victory" ending in a movie? Just because we believe a problem has been solved, doesn't mean it isn't ready to come back and fight us again! Is there something we can do to be prepared?

In the face of repeated revelations from God about the future of Abraham and Sarah, Abraham lied to Abimelech and nearly traded away Sarah's purity a second time to save his own skin. God stepped in, and saved the purity of Sarah and elevated Abraham in spite of his headstrong disobedience. Our text opens with the next scene.

Key Principle: God may bring back a long dead problem to strip me down – but He will use it to direct me to my proper place and unfold His promises to me!

I want to talk about God's hand in the midst of our troubles, but first we must set the scene to understand the context of Hagar's issues in the face of Sarah and Abraham's blessings. Let's zoom in to a collection of tents on the edge of a desert nearly four thousand years ago...

Setting the Scene: Genesis 21:1-8

It was a time of outlandish blessing: *Genesis 21:1* **Then** *the LORD took note of Sarah as He had said, and the LORD did for Sarah as He had promised. 2 So Sarah conceived and bore a son to Abraham in his old age, at the appointed time of which God had spoken to him. Then the Lord took note."*

Abraham's unreliability makes delay a risk to Sarah; however, the Lord had promised to bring the child that year.

Genesis 18:10 He said, "I will surely return to you at this time next year; and behold, Sarah your wife will have a son." And Sarah was listening at the tent door, which was behind him.

"As He had promised" - (*k'asher devar:* literally "because of the thing He had spoken.") God's Word is absolutely reliable.

It was a time of absolute confirmation: *Genesis 20:3 Abraham called the name of his son who was born to him, whom Sarah bore to him, Isaac. The name LAUGHTER was both a memory of faithlessness and rebuke, as well as a perfect name for the elation Sarah was feeling.*

God instructed the name: *Genesis 17:16 "I will bless her, and indeed I will give you a son by her. Then I will bless her, and she shall be a mother of nations; kings of peoples will come from her..." 19 But God said, "No, but Sarah your wife will bear you a son, and* **you shall call his name Isaac***; and I will establish My covenant with him for an everlasting covenant for his descendants after him."*

The laughter had a "story" of faithlessness buried in it. *Genesis 18:11 Now Abraham and Sarah were old, advanced in age; Sarah was past childbearing. 12 Sarah laughed to herself, saying, "After I have become old, shall I have pleasure, my lord being old also?" 13 And the LORD said to Abraham, "Why did Sarah laugh, saying, 'Shall I indeed bear a child, when I am so old?' 14 Is anything too difficult for the LORD? At the appointed* time I will return to you, at this time next year, and Sarah will have a son." 15 Sarah denied it however, saying, "I did not laugh," for she was afraid. And He said, "No, but you did laugh."

It is probably a good time to stop and make a note here on "**PERFECT FAITH.**" Romans 4 offers an interesting summary of Abraham's movements as he faced the promise of Isaac.

Romans 4:13 For the promise to Abraham or to his descendants that he would be heir of the world was not through the Law, but through the righteousness of faith. ..18 In hope against hope he believed, so that he might become a father of many nations according to that which had been spoken, "SO SHALL YOUR DESCENDANTS BE." 19 Without becoming weak in faith he contemplated his own body, now as good as dead since he was about a hundred years old, and the deadness of Sarah's womb; 20 yet, with respect to the promise of God, he did not waver in unbelief but grew strong in faith, giving glory to God, 21 and being fully assured that what God had promised, He was able also to perform. 22 Therefore IT WAS ALSO CREDITED TO HIM AS RIGHTEOUSNESS.

It is possible to read the words of Paul and lose the essential point he as making. You can read his words as though Abraham never wavered for a moment. That isn't true – and that isn't what he was really trying to say. Abraham was like the rest of us who believe. He had waves of doubt that assailed him. A reading of Genesis makes that observation obvious. Yet, he ultimately shaped his life around the truth of God's promises based on the Word of God stated to him.

I mention this to ease the sting of the notion of a one-time barbed hook of faith. We mature and learn to trust God. When we reflect back on the Biblical heroes, we have a tendency to make them bigger than life and better than we can be. That is not God's view. He offered the men, warts and all, to show us the truth of what He can do in the flimsy form of a man who will cling, as best he is able, to the powerful hand of an awesome God.

The Bible does not celebrate the sinner, but the Savior. Take heart! As Paul echoed: "I can do all things through HIM who strengthens me!"

It was a time of exacting obedience: *Genesis 21:4 Then Abraham circumcised his son Isaac when he was eight days old, as God had commanded him. 5 Now Abraham was* **one hundred years old** *when his son Isaac was born to him.*

A year before, God instructed and Abraham obeyed the circumcision rite for his own body, as well as Ishmael – who was about the time of puberty. God called upon Abraham to do it as a marker for his covenant, and Abraham was not about to "drop the ball" on this!

Genesis 17:24 Now Abraham was ninety-nine years old when he was circumcised in the flesh of his foreskin. 25 And Ishmael his son was thirteen years old when he was circumcised in the flesh of his foreskin. 26 In the very same day Abraham was circumcised, and Ishmael his son.

It was a time of deep fulfillment: *Genesis 21:6 Sarah said, "God has made laughter for me; everyone who hears will laugh with me." 7 And she said, "Who would have said to Abraham that Sarah would nurse children? Yet I have borne him a son in his old age." 8 The child grew and was weaned, and Abraham made a great feast on the day that Isaac was weaned.*

There is absolutely no doubt in my mind that the birth of Isaac was the most deeply fulfilling experience of Sarah's life. Her marriage was not unhappy, but nothing compared for a woman of the Biblical period to bearing a son to her husband. Sarah's aged body sprang to life, and she saw God work a miracle in her own body. There was never a healing with more exuberance, nor a deeper emotionally satisfying moment in her life. She would cherish this child. She would protect him with her life. **She loved his tiny little fingers and smooth skin more than anything she had ever held!**

Facing the Sting: Genesis 21:9-16

As strange as it may seem, the center of this episode is not Abraham nor Sarah, but the maid Hagar. She is the person in the passage that will both experience great and unexpected pain, and will see the intervention of God to renew her flagging spirit.

Hagar wasn't the cause of the struggle: 21:9 Now Sarah saw the son of Hagar the Egyptian, whom she had borne to Abraham, mocking. 10 Therefore she said to Abraham, "Drive out this maid and her son, for the son of this maid shall **not be an heir with** my son Isaac."

The term "mocking" (*m'tse-heck*: to play with) may mean the fourteen year old Ishmael was "picking on" Isaac, making fun of him. It may mean that he was simply playing with the little child. It could have been the roughness of the play that concerned Sarah. We simply don't know. **What we do know is that HAGAR was not involved this time.**

Hagar crossed Sarah before and paid a price for it. It was God alone that brought her back with Ishmael safely.

Genesis 16:6 But Abram said to Sarai, "Behold, your maid is in your power; do to her what is good in your sight." So Sarai treated her harshly, and she fled from her presence. 7 Now the angel of the LORD found her by a spring of water in the wilderness, by the spring on the way to Shur. 8 He said, "Hagar, Sarai's maid, where have you come from and where are you going?" And she said, "I am fleeing from the presence of my mistress Sarai." 9 Then the angel of the LORD said to her, "Return to your mistress, and submit yourself to her authority." 10 Moreover, the angel of the LORD said to her, "I will greatly multiply your descendants so that they will be too many to count."

It appears the JEALOUSY that poisoned Sarah and Hagar's relationship before resurfaced in the comment "not be an heir with" Isaac. Hagar probably thought that she was SAFE – since the angel instructed her to come back and directed the Word that her son was going to be great.

The point is that Hagar didn't see this coming at her again. She was blindsided by an old fit of jealousy.

Abraham didn't do the expected thing: The text is clear that Abraham didn't want to let Hagar go with Ishmael, as he loved his son deeply. The text offers only this: *Genesis 21:11 The matter distressed Abraham greatly because of his son.*

Abraham was not anxious to let Sarah decide this time as he had years before in Ishmael's infancy. This time his heart was tied up in the boy! Abraham's daily interactions with Ishmael probably offered a level of comfort to Hagar, and it was another reason she never dreamed she would be OUT of the tent again! She was SURE this problem would not revisit her, because Abraham would put his foot down... And then he didn't! She likely didn't know about God's intervention...

*Genesis 21:12 But God said to Abraham, "Do not be distressed because of the lad and your maid; **whatever Sarah tells you, listen to her**, for through Isaac your descendants shall be named. 13 And of the son of the maid I will make a nation also, because he is your descendant."*

How incredibly confusing! Listening to Sarah got Abe in very hot water the last time he did it! This cannot be! Yet it was God's command. He let go and let God do His thing....

Genesis 21:14 So Abraham rose early in the morning and took bread and a skin of water and gave them to Hagar, putting them on her shoulder, and gave her the boy, and sent her away. And she departed and wandered about in the wilderness of Beersheba.

God seemed to have abandoned her and His promises: Frankly, it couldn't have seemed any other way. God told her that her son would be the father of a great nation. God told her to go home. God told her to trust Him. She obeyed, and now was entirely shafted in spite of her obedience. What a great lesson!

The story offers an even more specific sense of the drama. She was alone in the heat of the desert with a child. Her canteen dried up, and she told her son to sit in the shade of a bush. She probably looked confidently at him, and said something like: "I will be back with more water. Do not leave! You must obey or we will both die. I cannot chase away and find you." Telling a young teen something like this was no doubt difficult, but she had much more experience than he in the desert. The text offers:

Genesis 21:15 When the water in the skin was used up, she left the boy under one of the bushes. 16 Then she went and sat down opposite him, about a bowshot away, for she said, "Do not let me see the boy die." And she sat opposite him, and lifted up her voice and wept.

She turned away so he could not hear her wail. The desert ate the sound. He sat under the bush waiting. Only a few days before he played before his father; now he was an outcast. He was hot and thirsty, and he was alone. Did he know how close to death they both were? Maybe, but Momma appeared to be working things out. The text says that he eventually began to cry...A few hundred feet away, Hagar reached the **despair** point.

Where was God? Why did He tell her that her child was so important? Did she ever really hear the words of the angel so long ago? Was her belief all a worthless lot?

It is worth noting that God waited in her silence and allowed her to pass all the way into despair before He answered her broken heart. He was not being cruel; He had a point to make. HE WOULD TAKE CARE OF THEM WITH HIS OWN HAND.

Finding the Promise - Genesis 21:17-21: God's Work in the Midst of Trouble

Here is the heart of our lesson. The text offers **seven truths** about **God's meeting with us in the crisis place**. Each truth moves us along from **isolation** to **blessing**:

Truth One: The Perception of God precedes our understanding: *Genesis 21:17a God heard the lad crying.* We may feel alone, but God hears our crying. He knows where we are and how we got there. The tears of painful isolation are a tool in His tool chest to help us learn that there are no "**God forsaken**" places. When the sons of Israel were enslaved and in misery – God heard them. The context of the statement is often used in the Torah for the words to care for strangers.

The Torah repeated the instruction to care for the stranger at least 33 times, far more than any other commandment. God told His people to be sensitive to the cry of others in their midst, as they had been oppressed. Those statements follow the pattern of God's dealing with the outcasts - Hagar and Ishmael.

The point here is that **God may use my life as a model** for someone or something that follows my short sojourn of the planet. I may not know why events happen – it may be centuries before the real reasons come out. As Naomi learned later, I must learn to trust God's character and follow God's Word in spite of what I see. He SEES WHAT I DO NOT AND HEARS, even when I may not feel He is listening!

Truth Two: The Perspective of God is expressed in His Word: *Genesis 21:17b "...and the angel of God called to Hagar from Heaven ..."* God's perspective on things as expressed in His Word is not at all like ours. He sees from above what we cannot see below. **From above, the end is seen at the beginning. From above, the purposes are clear without the blinding fog of the fallen nature.**

Truth Three: The Proclamations of God calls us to attend to HIS VOICES and HIS CHOICES: *Genesis 21:17b ...and said to her, "What is the matter with you (mah lach: What to you?), Hagar?* In the presence of God, we are urged to answer for ourselves – where we are and what we are doing. This is the first step to pressing us toward seeing HIS PLAN for us.

There was a fable of a dog who just could not stand for another dog to get the best of him in any way. One day the dog came across a large juicy steak that had somehow fallen off a meat wagon. He picked up the steak and started running with it. All was going well until he started across a bridge with water underneath. He noticed, there under the bridge was another dog with a big juicy steak in his mouth. He began to growl at the dog, and it looked as though the dog was growling back at him. He got so upset that he went to bark at the dog, and when he opened his mouth, the steak fell out into the river and sank to the bottom never to be seen again. Only then did he recognize he was looking at a reflection of himself in the water!

God may need to move us to a place where we are unable to see anything but HIM as our way of escape, in order that we may see clearly!

Truth Four: The Power of God extends into our specific weaknesses and needs: *Genesis 21:17 ...Do not fear, for God has heard the voice of the **lad where he is**.*

One New Year's Day, in the Tournament of Roses parade, a beautiful float suddenly sputtered and quit. It was out of gas. The whole parade was held up until someone could get a can of gas. The amusing thing was this float represented the Standard Oil Company. With its vast oil resources, its truck was out of gas. Often, Christians neglect their spiritual maintenance, and though they are "clothed with power" (Luke 24:49) find themselves out of gas. (Steve Blankenship in *God Came Near* by Max Lucado, Multnomah Press, 1987, p. 95)

Truth Five: The Promises of God offer us a hopeful future: 21:18 Arise, lift up the lad, and hold him by the hand, for I will make a great nation of him. You can't break God's promises by leaning on them! (Source Unknown)

A promise from God is a statement we can depend on with absolute confidence. Here are 12 promises for the Christian to claim:

- God's presence -- "I will never leave thee." (Heb. 13:5)
- God's protection -- "I am thy shield." (Gen. 15:1)
- God's power -- "I will strengthen thee." (Isa. 41:10)
- God's provision -- "I will help thee" (Isa. 41:10)
- God's leading -- "And when He puts forth His own sheep, He goes before them." (John 10:4)

Reading the Map: Lessons in Genesis

- God's purposes -- "I know the thoughts that I think toward you, says the Lord, thoughts of peace, and not of evil." (Jer. 20:11)
- God's rest -- "Come unto Me, all ye that labor and are heavy laden, and I will give you rest." (Matt. 11:28)
- God's cleansing -- "If we confess our sins, He is faithful and just to forgive us our sins, and to cleanse us from all unrighteousness." (1 John 1:9)
- God's goodness -- "No good thing will He withhold from them that walk uprightly." (Psalm 84:11)
- God's faithfulness -- "The Lord will not forsake His people for His great name's sake." (1 Sam. 12:22)
- God's guidance -- "The meek will He guide." (Psalm 25:9)
- God's wise plan -- "All things work together for good to them that love God." (Rom. 8:28) (*Our Daily Bread*, January 1, 1985)

Truth Six: The Provision of God is assured when we follow His plan: *Genesis 21:19 Then God opened her eyes and she saw a well of water; and she went and filled the skin with water and **gave the lad** a drink.*

"Abundance isn't God's provision for me to live in luxury, but his provision for me *to help others live."*

Truth Seven: The Presence of God establishes His plan in us: *Genesis 21:20 God was with the lad, and he grew; and he lived in the wilderness and became an archer. 21 He lived in the wilderness of Paran, and his mother took a wife for him from the land of Egypt.*

"An incident which happened on the battle front illustrates the fact that Christ has not deserted us in the battle, even at times when we feel all alone. King Victor Emmanuel III of Italy had gone with his troops into battle. In the midst of shell fire, a lieutenant who had fallen, mortally wounded, called a soldier, gave him a few keepsakes to convey to his family, and then ordered him to fly. But the soldier tried to carry the lieutenant to a place of safety. Some gunners called to him through the infernal fire: "Save yourself! Save yourself!" But still he remained. In the distance a motor horn could be heard, and the whisper went around that the king had left the field. The soldier still struggled with the officer's body, but the lieutenant died in his arms. Flinging himself on the corpse, the young fellow exclaimed with tears: "Even the king has gone away!" Then a hand touched his shoulder. He shook himself, rose, and stood at attention. "My dear boy," said the king, "the car has gone; but the king is still with you." And, there he remained till the end of the day." (*Youth's Companion*)

Just because we believe a problem has been solved, doesn't mean it isn't ready to come back and fight us again! There IS something we can do to be prepared - Watch Out! The villain you think you have defeated may not be as dead as you think. The problem you believe is solved may well come back for another run. **Be aware that a long dead problem may resurface – but God can use it to direct us to our proper place and unfold His promises to us – if we are listening and watching for Him!**

Reading the Map:
Lessons in Genesis

Lesson Twenty-one: Genesis 21:22-34
"Seven Character Traits of A Mature Believer"

With the last ballot cast in the election of 1860, Abraham Lincoln was elected to the Presidency of the United States. His 1.9 million popular votes was not a majority (only about 40% of the votes went to him), but his electoral vote was a landslide of 180 votes. Within two months the Union would be broken and the nation plunged into Civil War.

As the graduating class of West Point military academy had there silhouettes placed into frames, many of the handsome young soldiers carried this picture home on the brief stop before they left to fight. A big test was coming, they could feel it. For the moment, they paused and marked their lives with a picture. It became what one poet called "The Silhouette of the Ready Soldier."

Key Principle: The character traits of a mature believer are measurable and defined.

Character traits of a mature believer:

First, they build a healthy testimony before others (21:22)

Genesis 21:22 Now it came about at that time that Abimelech and Phicol, the commander of his army, spoke to Abraham, saying, "God is with you in all that you do..."

Note that God built a testimony in Abraham's life before these ungodly men. They encountered God when He rescued Sarah from their hands, in spite of the dishonesty of Abraham. **The testimony of a believer is normally built on his behavior**. In this case, it was based solely on the encounter they had with God on his behalf!

At the county fair a distinctively dressed Quaker offered a horse for sale. A non-Quaker farmer asked its price, and since Quakers had a reputation for fair dealing, he bought the horse without hesitation. The farmer got the horse home, only to discover it was lazy and ill-tempered, so he took it back to the fair the next day. There he confronted the Quaker.

"Thou hast no complaint against me," said the Quaker. "Had thou asked me about the horse, I would have told thee truthfully the problems, but thou didst not ask."

"That's okay," replied the farmer. "I don't want you to take the horse back. I want to try to sell him to someone else. Can I borrow your coat and hat awhile?" (Source Unknown)

David, the Psalmist, reminds us that God chooses, at times, to so mark the lives of believers that others cannot help but see His hand upon them. He desired that those who turned on Him would see God's hand in this life and be ashamed of their misdeeds.

*Psalm 86: 14 O God, arrogant men have risen up against me, and a band of violent men have sought my life, and they have not set You before them. 15 But You, O Lord, are a God merciful and gracious, slow to anger and abundant in lovingkindness and truth. 16 Turn to me, and be gracious to me; oh grant Your strength to Your servant, and save the son of Your handmaid. 17 Show me a sign for good, **that those who hate me may see it and be ashamed**, because You, O LORD, have helped me and comforted me.*

Many years ago the Douglas Aircraft company was competing with Boeing to sell Eastern Airlines its first big jets. War hero Eddie Rickenbacker, the head of Eastern Airlines, reportedly told Donald Douglas that the specifications and claims made by Douglas's company for the DC-8 were close to Boeing's on everything except noise suppression. Rickenbacker then gave Douglas one last chance to out-promise Boeing on this feature. After consulting with his engineers, Douglas reported that he didn't feel he could make that promise. Rickenbacker replied, "I know you can't, I just wanted to see if you were still honest." (*Today in the Word*, MBI, October, 1991, p. 22)

Second, they root their life in the truth (Genesis 21:23)

*Genesis 21:23 Now therefore, swear to me here by God that you will **not deal falsely** with me or with my offspring or with my posterity…*

God made His hand obvious in Abraham's life, but that did not imply to Abimelech and Phicol that such power would translate into a good relationship with him. They invited Abraham into a pact to attempt to induce him into a pact to gain any overflow blessing they could – and at the same time not incur any undue wrath of God for mistreating His people.

Both ideas are taught in the Word:

a. Blessing comes to those who bless God's people. In the literal sense, Abraham was the most obvious inheritor of such a promise. Gen. 12: 3 And I will **bless** those who bless you, and the one who **curses** you I will curse. And in you all the families of the Earth will be blessed.

b. In a general sense, the same is true of all believers. 1 Cor. 7:14 For the unbelieving husband is sanctified through his wife, and the unbelieving wife is sanctified through her believing husband; for otherwise your children are unclean, but now they are holy.

    2 Thessalonians 1:6-9 argues a curse upon those who cursed the people of God in the body of Christ at Thessaloniki.: *For after all it is only just for God to repay with affliction those who afflict you, 7 and to give relief to you who are afflicted and to us as well when the Lord Jesus will be revealed from Heaven with His mighty angels in flaming fire, 8 dealing out retribution to those who do not know God and to those who do not obey the gospel of our Lord Jesus. 9 These will pay the penalty of eternal destruction, away from the presence of the Lord and from the glory of His power.*

The believer should root out a lie in the truth, rather than follow after twisted words. Mature believers are to pick out the "unstable" teaching voices (*asteriktos*: not as it appears – 2 Peter 3.

We should be people that speak forthrightly what we mean. Jesus reminded us in *Matthew 5:37, But let your statement be, 'Yes, yes ' or 'No, no'; anything beyond these is of evil.*

Once, when a stubborn disputer seemed unconvinced, Lincoln said, "Well, let's see how many legs has a cow?" "Four, of course," came the reply disgustedly. "That's right," agreed Lincoln. "Now suppose you call the cow's tail a leg; how many legs would the cow have?" "Why, five, of course," was the confident reply. "Now, that's where you're wrong," said Lincoln. "Calling a cow's tail a leg doesn't make it a leg." (*Bits and Pieces,* July, 1991)

People don't say what they mean... Writing letters of recommendation can be hazardous. Tell the truth and you might get sued if the contents are negative. Robert Thornton, a professor at Lehigh University, has a collection of "virtually litigation-proof" phrases called the *Lexicon of Intentionally Ambiguous Recommendations,* or LIAR. Here are some examples:

- To describe an inept person--"I enthusiastically recommend this candidate with no qualifications whatsoever."

- To describe an ex-employee who had problems getting along with fellow workers--"I am pleased to say that this candidate is a former colleague of mine."

- To describe an unproductive candidate--"I can assure you that no person would be better for the job."

- To describe an applicant not worth consideration--" I would urge you to waste no time in making this candidate an offer of employment." (Larry Pryor in *Los Angeles Times*)

In business we must walk in truth:

Leviticus 19:36 You shall have just balances, just weights, a just ephah (dry), and a just hin (liquid); I am the LORD your God, Who brought you out from the land of Egypt.

Proverbs 20:10 Differing weights and differing measures, both of them are abominable to the LORD.

Two brothers were getting ready to boil some eggs to color for Easter. "I'll give you a dollar if you let me break three of these on your head," said the older one. "Promise?" asked the younger. "Promise!" Gleefully, the older boy broke two eggs over his brother's head. Standing stiff for fear the gooey mess would get all over him, the little boy asked, "When is the third egg coming?" "It's not," replied the brother. "That would cost me a dollar." (*Source Unknown*)

In our word we must speak truth: *Proverbs 24:26 (NIV) An honest answer is like a kiss on the lips.*

One reminded: "Those that think it permissible to tell white lies soon grow colorblind." (Austin O'Malley)

"Dr. Clarence Bass, professor emeritus at Bethel Theological Seminary, early in his ministry preached in a church in Los Angeles. He thought he had done quite well as he stood at the door greeting people as they left the sanctuary. The remarks about his preaching were complimentary. That is, until a little old man commented, "You preached too long." Dr. Bass wasn't fazed by the remark, especially in light of the many positive comments. "You didn't preach loud enough," came another negative comment. It was from the same little old man. Dr. Bass thought it strange that the man had come through the line twice, but when the same man came through the line a third time and exclaimed, "You used too many big words" --this called for some explanation. Dr. Bass sought out a deacon who stood nearby and asked him, "Do you see that little old man over there? Who is he?" "Don't pay any attention to him," the deacon replied. "All he does is go around and *repeats everything he hears.*" (*Pulpit and Bible Study Helps*, Vol.16, #5, p. 1)

Third, they work on relationships throughout the span of life (Genesis 21:23b)

Reading the Map: Lessons in Genesis

*Genesis 21:23b "...but according to the **kindness** that I have shown to you, **you shall show to me** and to the land in which you have sojourned. What Phicol and Abimelech wanted was a reciprocation of kindness.*

The standard of the heart Jesus **called on for a believer was clarified to be even greater**...

Luke 6: 27 But I say to you who hear, love your enemies, do good to those who hate you, 28 bless those who curse you, pray for those who mistreat you. 29 Whoever hits you on the cheek, offer him the other also; and whoever takes away your coat, do not withhold your shirt from him either. 30 Give to everyone who asks of you, and whoever takes away what is yours, do not demand it back. 31 Treat others the same way you want them to treat you. 32 If you love those who love you, what credit is that to you? For even sinners love those who love them. 33 If you do good to those who do good to you, what credit is that to you? For even sinners do the same. 34 If you lend to those from whom you expect to receive, what credit is that to you? Even sinners lend to sinners in order to receive back the same amount. 35 But love your enemies, and do good, and lend, expecting nothing in return; and your reward will be great, and you will be sons of the Most High; for He Himself is kind to ungrateful and evil men. 3 Be merciful, just as your Father is merciful.

We can live only in relationships. We need each other. A rather crude and cruel experiment was carried out by Emperor Frederick, who ruled the Roman Empire in the thirteenth century. He wanted to know what man's original language was: Hebrew, Greek, or Latin? He decided to isolate a few infants from the sound of the human voice. He reasoned that they would eventually speak the natural tongue of man. Wet nurses who were sworn to absolute silence were obtained, and though it was difficult for them, they abided by the rule. The infants never heard a word -- not a sound from a human voice. Within several months they were all dead. (Joe E. Trull.)

Single men are jailed more often, earn less, have more illnesses and die at a younger age than married men. Married men with cancer live 20% longer than single men with the same cancer. Women, who often have more close friendships than men, survive longer with the same cancers. Married or not, relationships keep us alive. (Dr. Bernie Siegel, *Homemade*, May, 1989)

Marian Anderson once performed at a concert in a small Nebraska college town. A student who was working her way through college was terribly disappointed when she could not get time off from her job at the local hotel desk to attend the concert. The great contralto was staying at the hotel, and after the concert she entered the lobby and went to the desk to see if there were any messages. The student inquired about the concert and expressed her disappointment that she had not been there. Marian Anderson stepped back, and there in the hotel lobby, unaccompanied, sang for the student. (*Ave Maria. Bits & Pieces*, May, 1991, p. 18)

Fourth, they stand consistently by their commitments (Genesis 21:24)

Genesis 21:24 Abraham said, "I swear it."

The fact is, you must get involved to have an impact. "No one is impressed with the "won-lost" record of the referee." (John H. Holcomb, *The Militant Moderate* [Rafter]) Abraham needed to commit verbally, then stand by the commitment.

"When Julius Caesar landed on the shores of Britain with his Roman legions, he took a bold and decisive step to ensure the success of his military venture. Ordering his men to march to the edge of the Cliffs of Dover, he commanded them to look down at the water below. To their amazement, they saw every ship in which they had crossed the channel engulfed in flames. Caesar had deliberately cut off any possibility of retreat. Now that his soldiers were unable to return to the continent, there was nothing left for them to do but to advance and conquer! And that is exactly what they did." (*Sermon Central Illustrations*)

I am convinced that many believers won't burn the bridges to their bad habits and previous life because they aren't truly sure they can be committed to God and His Word, and want a "back door" to retreat back into their old pattern of life.

We have to burn the bridges of bad habits and patterns and push ahead in our new lives!

On a recent trip to Haiti, I heard a Haitian pastor illustrate to his congregation the need for total commitment to Christ. His parable: A certain man wanted to sell his house for $2,000. Another man wanted very badly to buy it, but because he was poor, he couldn't afford the full price. After much bargaining, the owner agreed to sell the house for half the original price with just one stipulation: He would retain ownership of one small nail protruding from just over the door. After several years, the original owner wanted the house back, but the new owner was unwilling to sell. So the first owner went out, found the carcass of a dead dog, and hung it from the single nail he still owned. Soon the house became unlivable, and the family was forced to sell the house to the owner of the nail.

The Haitian pastor's conclusion: "If we leave the Devil with even one small peg in our life, he will return to hang his rotting garbage on it, making it unfit for Christ's habitation." (Dale A. Hays, *Leadership, Vol. X, No. 3* [Summer, 1989] p. 35)

Fifty-six men signed the Declaration of Independence. Their conviction resulted in untold sufferings for themselves and their families. Of the 56 men, five were captured by the British and tortured before they died. Twelve had their homes ransacked and burned. Two lost their sons in the Revolutionary Army. Another had two sons captured.   Nine of
the fifty-six fought and died from wounds or hardships of the war. Carter Braxton of Virginia, a wealthy planter and trader, saw his ships sunk by the British navy. He sold his home and properties to pay his debts and died in poverty. At the Battle of Yorktown, the British General Cornwallis had taken over Thomas Nelson's home for his headquarters. Nelson quietly ordered General George Washington to open fire on the Nelson home. The home was destroyed and Nelson died bankrupt. John Hart was driven from his wife's bedside as she was dying. Their thirteen children fled for their lives. His fields and mill were destroyed. For over a year, he lived in the forest and caves,

returning home only to find his wife dead and his children vanished. A few weeks later, he died from exhaustion. (Kenneth L. Dodge, *Resource,* Sept./ Oct., *1992,* p. 5)

Fifth, they face problems realistically and directly (Genesis 21:25-26)

Genesis 21:25 But Abraham **complained** *to Abimelech because of the well of water which the servants of Abimelech had seized. 26 And Abimelech said, "I do not know who has done this thing; you did not tell me, nor did I hear of it until today."*

"Abraham complained" is actually the term he "argued" (from *yawkach*). He was prepared to make an agreement, but not without disclosing any outstanding issues that would not be appropriate. Believers are not called to be suckers that just say "yes" to any agreement. He wanted to press a case for the injustice being done to his men. That is appropriate.

Matthew Henry stated: "The faults of servants must not be imputed to their masters, unless they know of them and justify them; and no more can be expected from an honest man than that he be ready to do right as soon as he knows that he has done wrong.

In time, and as one comes to benefit from experience, *one learns that things will turn out neither as well as one hoped nor as badly as one feared.* (Jerome S. Bruner, *Bits and Pieces,* November, 1989, p. 17)

It is neither sour, nor wrong to connect the cause and effect of problems – it is realism in the proper sense. Take for example:

Surveys in 1986:

- 70% of high school grads leave the church, never to return
- 65% of evangelical teens never read their Bibles
- 33% believe religion is out of date and out of touch
- 40% of all teens believe in astrology
- 30% read astrology column daily
- 93% know their sign

- 58% of protestant teens believe students should have access to contraceptives
- 25% of high school students contract some form of V.D.
- 42% of protestant teens say there are many ways to God
- 60% question that miracles are possible
- 28% feel the content of the Bible are not accurate

THEN... According to surveys in 1990:

- 65% of all H.S. Christian students are sexually active
- 75% of all H.S. students cheat regularly
- 30% of all H.S. students have shoplifted in the past 30 days
- 45-50% of all teen pregnancies are aborted
  - million teens are alcoholics
- 1000 teens try to commit suicide daily
- 10% of H.S. students have experimented with or are involved in a homosexual lifestyle. (Bruce Wilkinson, 7 Laws of the Learner).

Sixth, they are very deliberate about boundaries (Genesis 21:27-32)

*Genesis 21:27 Abraham took sheep and oxen and gave them to Abimelech, and the two of them made a **covenant**. 28 Then Abraham set seven ewe lambs of the flock by themselves. 29 Abimelech said to Abraham, "What do these seven ewe lambs mean, which you have set by themselves?" 30 He said, "You shall take these seven ewe lambs from my hand so that it may be a witness to me, that I **dug this well**." 31 Therefore he called that place Beersheba, because there the two of them took an oath. 32 So they made a covenant at Beersheba; and Abimelech and Phicol, the commander of his army, arose and returned to the land of the Philistines.*

Matthew Henry again offers a word: "He took care to have his title to the well cleared and confirmed, to prevent any disputes or quarrels for the future, v. 30. It is *justice*, as well as wisdom, to do thus, "*in perptuam rei memoriam*" that *the circumstance may be perpetually remembered.*"

Robert Schuller told an interesting story on an early broadcast of his TV show – a story that occurred years ago in San Diego. The elevator at the El Cortez Hotel could not handle the number of people who were staying at the hotel. The experts -- engineers and architects -- were called in. They decided to put another elevator in by cutting a hole in each floor and installing the motor for the new elevator in the basement. The plans were drawn up. Everything was in order. One day the architect and the engineer came into the lobby discussing their plans. A janitor, who was there with his mop, heard them say they were going to chop holes in the floors. The janitor said, "That's going to make a mess." The engineer said, "Of course. But we'll get help for you, don't worry." The janitor observed, "You'll have to close the hotel for a while." "Well, if we have to close the hotel for a while, we'll close the hotel. We must have another elevator." Holding his mop in his hand, the janitor asked, "Do you know what I would do if I were you?" The architect arrogantly responded, "What?" "I'd build the elevator on the outside," the janitor replied. The janitor's unique idea astonished the experts. But the elevator was built on the outside. This was the first time in the history of architecture that an elevator was built on the outside of a building.

We get so caught up in our thinking about our situations that we don't see it from another perspective. Abraham decided to try to be very open about what was going wrong, and then try to proactively deal with a symbol that would help everyone understand the property boundary. If they FORGOT, he gave them a REMINDER. He helped solve the problem with A NEW APPROACH to it.

Seven: They trust confidently in God's Promises (Genesis 21:33-34)

*Genesis 21:33 Abraham **planted a tamarisk tree** at Beersheba, and there he called on the name of the LORD, the **Everlasting God**. 34 And Abraham sojourned in the land of the Philistines for manydays.*

The famous Russian novelist Fyodor Dostoevsky told the story of the time he was arrested by the czar and sentenced to die. The czar, though, liked to play cruel psychological tricks on the people who rebelled against him by blindfolding them and standing them in front of a firing squad. The blindfolded people would hear the gunshots go off, but would feel nothing. Then they would slowly realize that the guns were loaded with blanks.

Dostoevsky went through this experience himself. He said that going through the process of dying, believing he was really going to die, had a transforming effect on Dostoevsky. He talked about waking up that morning with full assurance that this would be his last day of life. He ate his last meal and savored every bite. Every breath of air he took was precious to him. Every face he saw, he studied with full intensity. Suddenly, every experienced was etched in his mind.

As they marched him into the courtyard, he felt the heat of the sun and appreciated its warmth like never before. Everything around him seemed to have a magical quality to it. He was seeing the world in a way he had never seen it before. He was fully alive!

When he realized that he had not been shot and that he was not going to die, everything about his life changed. He became thankful for everything about his life. He became grateful to people he had previously hated. It was this experience that convinced him to become a novelist and write about life in a way that before would have never been known to him.

You see, Christians ought to be fully alive like this. We've stared death in the face. If you are a believer in Christ, then you came to the understanding at some point in your life that your sin would lead you to eternal death. We all were doomed to die. But ... God sent his Son Jesus Christ to die in our place, and because of that we live. And because of that – in view of God's mercy, Paul says – offer your bodies as living sacrifices. Live and give as fully alive people of God.

Reading the Map:
Lessons in Genesis

Lesson Twenty-two: Genesis 22:1-19
"The Grand Prize for the Great Surrender"

Following WWII, the crushed state of Imperial Japan was slowly and systematically advanced from a poor and starving nation, to a well-managed and prosperous one. Though no one would argue that Japan did not suffer terribly in the wake of the war, in the matter of a generation, the economy of Japan went from a "developing nation" status to a world class market economy.

Yet, not all Japanese benefited from this development – because they refused to surrender the war! If you "google" the "last surrender of a Japanese soldier from WWII" you will read some interesting stories.

- The last Japanese soldier to surrender was Captain Fumio Nakahira who held out until April, 1980, before being discovered at Mt. Halcon on Mindoro Island in the Philippines.

- Before that, Nakamura Teruo was discovered on the island of Morotai on December 18, 1974 - still believing the war was on.

- Sergeant Yoloi Shoichi survived in the jungles of Guam until found on January 24, 1972. He died in September, 1997 at the age of 82.

- The most famous one though, was Onoda Hiroo, who was discovered in the jungle of Lubang Island on March 11, 1974, twenty-nine years after the war ended. <u>He did not surrender his post until the Japanese government located his former commanding officer and sent him to call the man in from the jungle.</u>

Hiroo has since published a book *'No Surrender: My Thirty-Year War.'* Carrying on his private guerilla war for nearly thirty years, he <u>never lived the benefits of an entire generation of Japanese</u> that lived after the surrender. He didn't live in the prosperity of post-war Japan, with its booming industrial and technical economy. He missed it all fighting a war that was already over. He resisted alone, and never learned the prize of surrender. He hungered, thirsted, sacrificed, and lived alone – all for nothing.

Sadly, the same is true of many believers in the church today! They have **never truly surrendered** to the One Who victoriously loosed them from the tyranny of everlasting darkness and its prince. As a result, they *lack the prize that comes from true surrender*. To truly grasp this concept, God provided a model in His Word from the ancient record of Abraham the Patriarch. Long ago, **Abraham had a special moment in his life that revealed something about God he had never quite understood**...

Key Principle: When a believer surrenders completely to God, God fills his life with the greatest provision of all – Himself. It is an existence more satisfying than any other.

Today we will be able to clearly see that God has PRECONDITIONS for the great surrender test, shows us a PROCESS of how the test works, and how we should respond, and finally – and this is the main point of encouragement – the PRIZE of the great surrender test.

PRE-CONDITIONS OF THE GREAT SURRENDER TEST (Genesis 22:1a)

The lesson of full surrender is offered for whom? Should everyone be ready to lay down everything today, or is the lesson more specifically for SOME of us?

*Genesis 22:1 "Now it came about **after these things**, that **God tested Abraham**, and said to him...*

To **what** "things" is Genesis 22:1 referring? There are three prominent things in the Word. They are not DETAILS, for they provide the key to WHO IS IN VIEW to being presented with the test of ultimate surrender, for which God offers an unbeatable prize:

First, an initial dramatic recognition of God as Lord of his life: After the "**Great Exchange**" where God met for the first time with the young Abram and called him to leave Ur of the Chaldees to go to a land God would show him, he left what he knew for what he had not seen – in faith that God would bring him to the promised place (Genesis 12:1-3).

We need an encounter with God in which we decide to follow Him instead of the lost world, or the longings of our own fallen heart. We need an encounter with God that surrenders the **goal** of our life – leaving behind the serving of self for the serving of the Master. **Without that – nothing else matters.** This transformation happened when Abram stopped living life for himself, and began basing his life on the promise of God.

Today we refer to such an exchange as a "new birth," and like Abram, the **city of destination** is radically changed!

Second, a process of growth in understanding of the scope of God's promises:

- After a series of encounters with God he received special promises from God at each! Each promise of God came on the heels of some great step of obedience!

- After the "**Defining Promise**" of God, in a second meeting with God, He promised to give Abram a corps of descendants that would inherit all the physical property he could see in the center of the land later called "holy" by God (Genesis 12:7). This promise came AFTER Abram followed God and journeyed to the land.

- After the "**Extended Promise**" of God, in a third meeting with God when the land contract for his descendants was expanded to eternity, He gave an allotment that would be titled in perpetuity to them (Genesis 13:14).

- This promise came AFTER Abram learned a critical lesson in lying to Pharaoh of Egypt, and later journeyed to save Lot, his nephew, and

- Then offered tithes to the man of God, Melchisedek – lessons in properly and improperly caring for those under his protection (Sarai and Lot).

- After the "**Specifying Promise**" of God, in a fourth meeting with God recorded in Genesis 15:1-21, God opened the door to Abram and shared that Abram would himself have a vast number of descendants that would shape history. God revealed they would come from his own loins, and that they would inherit a land currently occupied by others.

- This promise came AFTER a time had passed when Abram languished over his unfruitful loins (15:1). God's promise of a future great nation was passed, but NOTHING WAS HAPPENING on the baby front, and Abram may well have believed God was not going to meet the desire and longing of his heart to have a son.

- After the "**Timing Promise**" of a fifth recorded meeting where God changed the now 99-year-old (17:1, 24) Abram's name to Abraham (17:5) and the 90-year-old Sarai's name to Sarah (17:15), God told him that He would not just bless the world through a people, but that NATIONS (plural) would come from him – *and HER- within the next year*!

- God identified the COVENANT was through Abraham, and the covenant symbol of circumcision was commanded to Abraham (17:1-21).

- This promise happened AFTER watching the young Ishmael grow for 13 years in their home tent, and was reaffirmed AFTER Abraham followed through on the circumcision of the entire household as a symbol in another meeting a short time later (Genesis 18) when Abraham pleaded for righteous men at Sodom.

We need encounters with the Word of God, where we comprehend His promises and His objectives in our life. This is the life of a growing believer.

Third, clear indications of God's unfailing grace amidst personal failures after the direct intervention of God to keep Sarah pure in spite of Abraham's lie to protect himself before the prince of Gerar (Genesis 20). This harkened back to a failure to learn the same lesson from years before in relation to believing God's promises and trusting God's protections (see Genesis 12:13- 20). The failures were meant with the strong hand of God's blessing in spite of Abraham's disobedience – a blessing that was apparent to anyone who observed his life (cp. Genesis 21:22).

We need to experience the blessing of God in spite of our own unfaithfulness, lest we believe we have what we have because we somehow deserve it. We need the failures to plague us with dark nights of the guilt of the soul, and wake up to a dawn of blessing that highlights the grace of a loving God.

Don't get lost in the details here, but don't skip the details either! **The three things we just looked at were conditions of what God unfolded before Abraham. They are conditions that set up the GREAT TEST of the passage.**

- God worked in Abraham after he met God in initial recognition of God's Lordship over his life. **This message of the prize of surrender is NOT (strictly speaking) a message about salvation – it is to those who KNOW GOD.** Abraham knew God. As a result, I am not suggesting that God is offering the prize of surrender (that we will define in a few moments) ONLY to those who have already acknowledged in their life that God is their rightful Master. Self-willed people who have rejected God as Lord and control their own lives – those who do not want a Savior because they believe they have no NEED of a Savior - are not in view for the prize of which I am speaking.

- Additionally, **NEW BELIEVERS do not seem to be in view here**. God offers the prize of supreme surrender to the believer that has had time to marinate in the promises of God. They know that God is working on their future, and that God has a plan for them. They have read the promises of God in His Word, and they have come to believe in them – though they are not always consistent in their actions.

- Finally, **PERFECT CHRISTIANS** are not in view here. God presented the test of surrender (and the prize that came from passing the test) to a believer who had **ample illustrations of his own personal failures and the abundant showing of God's mercy** and grace!

This message of the GREAT SURRENDER TEST and its prize has pre-conditions. God's test of surrender is for the **BELIEVER**, who HAS **GROWN IN THE PROMISES** of the Word of God. The test is for the one who **KNOWS THEIR UNFAITHFULNESS** and yet has **seen God LAY HIS HAND** on their life in spite of their failures. If that is YOU, the test may now be in front of you today….

VERSE 1 SAYS THAT GOD TESTED ABRAHAM, BUT…It wasn't a test so that God could find out the extent of Abraham's faith and devotion… God already knew - but *Abraham* didn't.

God doesn't test us for HIS LEARNING – But for OUR LEARNING. You can't prejudge your reaction until the moment of crisis arrives. **Only your character will determine the choice in the crisis moment.**

PROCESS OF THE GREAT SURRENDER TEST
(Genesis 22:1b-10)

Genesis 22:1b: … "Abraham!" And he said, "Here I am."

Method: The test begins with God personally dealing deep within the heart of the believer.

It is not a "group thing" but an individual encounter with God. It is not that such an encounter will not happen in a group meeting –

it could be happening right now. The simple truth is that it DOESN'T REQUIRE a group meeting – **it is a deeply personal issue between you and God.**

Believers that have a long walk with God should anticipate this test. **It will come.** When SCOTT PECK said, "Life is difficult. Once we truly know that life is difficult, once we truly understand and accept it, then life is no longer difficult," he offered a hint. Don't shy away from the great surrender test. It isn't there to daunt you or cause you to shrink – **it is there to provide you with a great prize!**

*Genesis 22:2 He said, "**Take now your son, your only son, whom you love, Isaac**, and go to the land of Moriah, and **offer him there** as a burnt offering on one of the mountains of which I will tell you."*

Message: The test is always about the singularly most important thing in our lives that has not been surrendered.

Note the way God addressed the issue. He said take "your son," "your ONLY son", the "one whom you love" – offer HIM. **Don't forget that God knew Abraham HAD ANOTHER SON – ISHMAEL. God knew that he loved Ishmael.** God knew he had already given up Ishmael with Hagar to a life away from his tent…The issue was that God knew what **Abraham cherished MORE than anything else in his life**.

God wanted to pointedly and clearly mark a circle around that ONE LOVE. For each of us it may be a different thing. For some it may be the hunger to be loved by others. For some it may be the longing of Hannah for a child from your own body. For some it may be the fleeting pleasures a fortune could afford. We all have our thing.

The message is – "I want the most important thing – the thing that you could set above ME," says the Lord. "Give it to Me."

Don't forget to notice that God specified WHAT to offer, WHERE, and WHEN to offer it. This test is not unclear in the mind – **You will know** what it is when God knocks on the door of your heart.

THE TRUTH IS THAT GOD GIVES US 'ISAACS' IN OUR LIFE – BUT THEY CAN BECOME 'IDOLS' IN HIS PLACE.

Gary Ezzo says that one of the problems with families today is that the husband & wife join hands to form a family circle. Then a child comes along & they place the child in the center, with the husband & wife still forming the circle. But now everything revolves around the child. Then a second child comes & that child is also placed inside the circle, with the husband & wife as the circle around them. And now everything revolves around the two children. As other children come along the center becomes so big that the hands of the father & mother are pulled apart & the family circle is broken. Ezzo says that what we must do is form the circle, but with Christ in the center. Then as each child is born, it joins hands with mom & dad to make the circle bigger. And the result is that the circle is never broken as long as Christ is the center. (Pastor Melvin Newland)

Dr. James Dobson in *Dare to Discipline*, says, Excessive love can be unhealthy for a child, just as the absence of love can destroy it. Excessive love can cause a child to be spoiled by love. We are so child-oriented today that the child becomes the center of virtually everything that goes on in our families. As a result, we make 3 costly mistakes with *excessive love*:

1. The first one is "overprotection."
2. The second costly mistake is "*overindulgence*," giving your child too much. Jesus said, "Watch out, be on guard against all kinds of greed, for a man's life does not consist in the abundance of his possessions."
3. The third costly mistake is "*over-permissiveness*."

Listen to Proverbs 29:17, **Discipline your son, & he will give you peace; he will bring delight to your soul**. Proverbs 13:24 says, **He who spares the rod hates his son, but he who loves him is careful to discipline him**.

Marks: The test is passed over a time – but the marks of progress are clear and notable.

SWIFT RESPONSE - *Genesis 22:3 So Abraham **rose early in the morning** and saddled his donkey...*There was **no delay** in the first steps to obedience – he got up the next morning *early*.

SILENT RESPONSE - *Genesis 22:3b "...and **took two of his young men with him and Isaac** his son; and he **split wood** for the burnt offering, and **arose and went** to the **place** of which God had told him.* He took the personal command deeply within and kept silent about it. He **did not debate it with others**.

Our faith is not truly stretched to its limit until God asks us to bear what seems unbearable, do what seems unreasonable, and expect what seems impossible. DO NOT FORGET THE INVISIBLE ONE IS ALSO THE INVINCIBLE ONE!

STEADY RESPONSE - *Genesis 22:4 On **the third day** Abraham raised his eyes and saw the place from a **distance**.* A few verses later, we can hear the background music reaching a crescendo as the dramatic moment approaches. All the while Abraham is steadily doing what God commanded!

Genesis 22:9 Then they came to the place of which God had told him; and Abraham built the altar there and arranged the wood, and bound his son Isaac and laid him on the altar, on top of the wood. 10 Abraham stretched out his hand and took the knife to slay his son." Abe had time to **reconsider**, but **refused** to allow the time to dissuade his determination to follow God.

WHERE is the GREAT PRIZE OF GOD found? It is found in the place of His assignment. We have no right to expect the provision of God if we are not in the place of His will.

SURE RESPONSE – Look in Genesis 22:5 *"Abraham said to his young men, "Stay here with the donkey, and **I and the lad will go** over there; and **we will worship and return** to you." 22:6 Abraham took the **wood** of the burnt offering and laid it on Isaac his son, and he **took** in his **hand the fire and the knife**. So the **two of them walked on together**. 7 Isaac spoke to Abraham his father and said, "My father!" And he said, "Here I am, my son." And he said, "Behold, the fire and the wood, but **where is***

*the lamb for the burnt offering?" 8 Abraham said, "**God will provide for Himself the lamb** for the burnt offering, my son."* So the two of them **walked on together**."

Abraham truly believed in the **ultimate promise** of God! Had not God said to him before: *Genesis 17:19 But God said, "No, but Sarah your wife will bear you a son, and you shall call his name Isaac; and I will establish My covenant with him for an everlasting covenant for his descendants after him."*

God's promises could only be TRUE if God was going to provide another way for Isaac to live after the sacrifice on the hill. **The "AND WE WILL WORSHIP AND WE WILL RETURN"** (ve·nish·ta·cha·veh ve·na·shu·vah a·lei·chem) **are some of the most profound words in Scripture. Abraham was declaring BEFORE THE TEST – God has a plan. It will be alright!**

How could Abraham believe that God would raise up his DEAD SON? (HEBREWS 11:17-19). Abraham believed that God could raise Isaac from the dead because he had already **personally experienced resurrection power** in his own body in order to *have* this child.

WHEN is the GREAT PRIZE found? In the process of His assignment: when we have the need and not a moment sooner. Abraham was obedient with hand in air when God moved on his behalf.

THE PRIZE OF THE GREAT SURRENDER TEST
(Genesis 22:11-19)

The moment of the great surrender test is CAREFULLY MONITORED by God.

*Genesis 22:11 But the **angel of the LORD called** to him from Heaven and said, "**Abraham, Abraham!**" And he said, "**Here I am**." 12 He said, "Do not stretch out your hand against the lad, and **do nothing to him**; for **now I know that you fear God**, since **you have not withheld your son**, your only son, from Me."*

Note that **you are not asked by an aloof God to lay it all on the altar.** He is not content to offer you standards and walk away. Your offer of the greatest thing is what He desires – offered faith that He knows how it will all come out.

Pastor Guy McGraw cites a Charles Stanley story: Charles Stanley's Grandfather: "If God says run your head through a brick wall and you take off running, God will put a hole there when you need it."(*Sermon Central.com Illustrations*)

The moment of the great surrender test QUICKLY STRIPS the blinders from men - God has it all in His hands.

*Genesis 22:13 **Then Abraham** raised his eyes and **looked,** and behold, behind him **a ram caught in the thicket** by his horns; and Abraham went and **took the ram and offered him up** for a burnt offering in the place of his son.*

Abraham saw for the first time the deep and enduring truth – that **God never calls a man or woman to provide anything for God. We aren't able to SUPPLY GOD with anything that He wants – except ourselves.** We can give but one thing – our true, wholehearted allegiance. Our honest surrender of that person, need or thing that is most cherished. That is the chief act of surrender.

Note how deeply God uttered the words "because you have not withheld" in the following verses.

Guy McGraw: Hudson Taylor's famous quote reminds us: "WHEN GOD'S WORK IS DONE GOD'S WAY IT WILL NEVER LACK GOD'S SUPPLY." The founder of the China Inland Mission used to hang in his home a plaque with two Hebrew Words on it: EBENEZER & JEHOVAH JIREH. They mean: 'Hitherto hath the Lord helped us' and 'The Lord will see to it or provide.' One looked back while the other looked forward. One reminded him of God's faithfulness and the other of God's assurances." (*sermoncentral.com*)

The moment of the great surrender test offers the CHIEF PRIZE of all – the intimate encounter with God's complete provision and personal care.

*Genesis 22:14 Abraham called the name of that place **The LORD Will Provide**, as it is said to this day, "In the mount of the LORD it will be provided." 15 Then the **angel** of the LORD **called** to Abraham **a second time from Heaven**, 16 and said, "By Myself I have sworn, declares the LORD, **because you have done this thing** and have **not withheld** your son, your only son, 17 indeed **I will greatly bless you**, and I will greatly **multiply** your **seed** as the stars of the heavens and as the sand which is on the seashore; and your **seed** shall **possess** the gate of their enemies. 18 In your **seed all the nations** of the Earth shall be **blessed, because you have obeyed My voice**." 19 So Abraham returned to his young men, and they arose and went together to Beersheba; and Abraham lived at Beersheba.*

I wonder if the reason we don't surrender fully, is because we don't understand the value of the prize!

When a believer surrenders completely to God, God fills his life with the greatest provision of all – **Himself. It is an existence more satisfying than any other. Do you suppose those Japanese soldiers that hadn't heard and believed the surrender order ever could conceive of how life had changed in Japan?** Did you ever really understand the **PRIZE** of **SURRENDER – NO - - because they missed it while keeping up the war. So can we if we aren't ready to surrender.**

Philip Yancey tells about an African safari he was on where he saw an old momma giraffe taking care of her offspring. Shortly after he was born she went over & kicked her offspring, & it looked like she was really hurting her baby. Then she did it again. Each time, the little giraffe would get up on his wobbly legs & try to walk. Still she continued kicking him. Finally, he got up pretty rapidly & ran away from her kicks.

Phil turned to his guide & asked, "Why does the mother giraffe do that?" The guide answered, "The only defense the giraffe has is its ability to get up quickly and to outrun its predator. If it can't do that, it will soon die."

Yancy said that while it looked like it was a cruel thing, it was really the most loving thing the mother could do for her offspring. And sometimes discipline is the same way.

Don't look at God as though His desire for your surrender is a sadistic and cruel thing. He knows we need Him to live. He alone can provide what we truly lack – that connection so cruelly severed at the Fall in the garden!

Reading the Map:
Lessons in Genesis

Lesson Twenty-three: Genesis 23
"Five Lessons from Painful Loss"

Loss is not designed to be a needlessly cruel exercise of a harsh God – though in the midst of the pain that is exactly what the enemy will shout into our lives. Theologians will attempt to parse God's original design and it will feel like an excuse and an unwanted exercise of sophistry when we are in the gripping pain of searing loss. Well-meaning believers, unsure of how to comfort us, will tell us how they understand the tearing we are going through – words we do not truly believe.

Every human relationship will feel like a failure to us in the time of intense grief – yet it is the time when God can most easily be heard. There is no other voice we need to hear – and no other voice can reach through a pain so deep – if we will listen for Him.

In the map of life outlined in the beginning of our *Bible*, LOSS must be addressed. We will all face it, and we will all need to know how to deal with it. God doesn't duck the hard things in His Word – He knows what we need... and we need lessons on LOSS.

This text is part of the cycle of Torah readings called "Chayei Sarah" (in Gen 23:1-25:11). Unlike Hollywood's recent release, "Three Weddings and A Funeral," we would call this Torah portion, "Two Funerals and a Wedding". The story revolves around the death of Sarah, setting the stage for Abraham to send his servant to find a wife for Isaac, and ends with the "passing of the family mantle of leadership to Isaac" with the death of Abraham. Rabbi's call this a "cycle of life" Torah portion, or may be better defined today as "times when your extended family gets together" portion... weddings and funerals.

The three stories are: 1) The death and burial of Sarah; 2) The search for and marriage to Isaac's bride; 3) The death and burial of Abraham. Each lesson presents some specific life and family lessons that God considered essential on the "Road Map" of the book of Genesis. Since the key player in the passage is Abraham, the key truths taught by the passage can be found by following HIM in the story…and lessons concerning his loss and how he faced those dark days.

Key Principle: Loss in this life is part of God's training ground for all of us.

There are FIVE LESSONS we want to encounter in this lessons:

First, the <u>Lesson of Unwarranted Futility</u>: Loss can make us want to give up – we must keep going for our whole journey here.

Genesis 23:1 Now Sarah lived one hundred and twenty-seven years; these were the years of the life of Sarah. 2 Sarah died in Kiriath-arba (that is, Hebron) in the land of Canaan; and Abraham went in to mourn for Sarah and to weep for her.

God only names the age of one woman upon her death, Sarah. One Rabbi said, "Even God knew it was wisest not to mention some things!"

Abraham lost the love of his life and the companion that traveled the whole journey with him. She was introduced in Genesis 11, at his side from his initial call by God.

Genesis 11:29b The name of Abram's wife was Sarai; …. 30 Sarai was barren; she had no child. 31 Terah took Abram his son, and Lot the son of Haran, his grandson, and Sarai his daughter-in-law, his son Abram's wife; and they went out together from Ur of the Chaldeans in order to enter the land of Canaan; and they went as far as Haran, and settled there.

The *Bible* reflected what was no doubt Abraham's heart view of Sarah -- **she had ALWAYS been there in the story of his life's journey.** I doubt he could remember what life was like before SHE was in the picture. She wasn't simply a piece of furniture in his life -- a comfy sofa. She was a **PLAYER** in all the major movements and decisions – she is mentioned BY NAME repeatedly.

Funerals invite retrospective looks. **Death makes life more precious. Moments tick by and we are called to take into account the limited number of them in stewarding God's good gifts**.

Moses sang out in Psalm 90:10: As for the days of our life, they contain seventy years, or if due to strength, eighty years. Yet their pride is but labor and sorrow; for soon it is gone and we fly away. 11 Who understands the power of Your anger and Your fury according to the fear that is due You? 12 So teach us to number our days, that we may present to You a heart of wisdom.

David echoed the idea in his song: Psalm 39: 4 LORD, make me to know my end and what is the extent of my days; let me know how transient I am. 5 Behold, You have made my days as handbreadths, and my lifetime as nothing in Your sight; surely everyman at his best is a mere breath.

Long ago, Matthew Henry, the Bible Commentator noted a truth: In our greatest health and prosperity every man is altogether vanity; he cannot live long; he may die soon. This is an undoubted truth, but we are very unwilling to believe it.

God's gift of the temporary nature of the physical part of our eternal life is a special gift to highlight the importance of stewarding well – since there is a real limitation to the time we spend on Earth in this body.

To understand the scene in Genesis 23 as Abraham experienced it, let's drift back in our hearts to what Abraham could recall. Sarah was his partner when:

- **God gave the call to the Promised Land**:

Genesis 12:5 Abram took Sarai his wife and Lot his nephew, and all their possessions which they had accumulated, and the persons which they had acquired in Haran, and they set

out for the land of Canaan; thus they came to the land of
Canaan.

- **Her husband shamed the family with a lie and poor
testimony before Pharaoh**:

*Genesis 12:10 Now there was a famine in the land;   so
Abram went down to Egypt to sojourn there, for the famine
was severe in the land. 11It came about when he came near
to Egypt, that he said to Sarai his wife, "See now, I know
that you are a beautiful woman; 12 and when the Egyptians
see you, they will say, 'This is his wife'; and they will kill me,
but they will let you live. 13 Please say that you are my sister
so that it may go well with me because of you, and that I
may live on account of you.*

- **She watched the struggles and eventual division in
her family**:

*Genesis 13:1 So Abram went up from Egypt to the Negev,
he and his wife and all that belonged to him, and Lot with
him… 5 Now Lot, who went with Abram, also had flocks and
herds and tents. 6 And the land could not sustain them while
dwelling together, for their possessions were so great that
they were not able to remain together. 7 And there was strife
between the herdsmen of Abram's livestock and the
herdsmen of Lot's livestock. Now the Canaanite and the
Perizzite were dwelling then in the land.*

- **She (fearfully, no doubt) watched her husband go off
to war for a just cause**:

*Genesis 14:14   When Abram heard that his relative had
been taken captive, he led out his trained men, born in his
house, three hundred and eighteen, and went in pursuit as
far as Dan. 16 He brought back all the goods, and also
brought back his relative Lot with his possessions, and also
the women, and the people.*

- **She stood by her husband during the deep pains and
doubts of his life**:

Genesis 15:2 Abram said, "O Lord GOD, what will You give me, since I am childless, and the heir of my house is Eliezer of Damascus?" 3 And Abram said, "Since You have given no offspring to me, one born in my house is my heir." 4 Then behold, the word of the LORD came to him, saying, "This man will not be your heir; but one who will come forth from your own body, he shall be your heir."

- **She felt pain over not being able to fulfill his desires, and tried to devise a way to add the joy he was missing**:

*Genesis 16:1 Now Sarai, Abram's wife had borne him no children, and she had an Egyptian maid whose name was Hagar. 2 So Sarai said to Abram, "Now behold, **the LORD has prevented me from bearing children**. Please go in to my maid; perhaps I will obtain children through her." And Abram listened to the voice of Sarai.*

- **She wrestled with her self- image and relationships that helped shape the whole family**:

Genesis 16:4b…when [Hagar] she saw that she had conceived, her mistress [Sarai] was despised in her sight. 5 And Sarai said to Abram, "May the wrong done me be upon you. I gave my maid into your arms, but when she saw that she had conceived, I was despised in her sight. May the LORD judge between you and me." 6 But Abram said to Sarai, "Behold, your maid is in your power; do to her what is good in your sight." So Sarai treated her harshly, and she fled from her presence.

God DID fulfill the longing of both Sarah and Abraham in Isaac. Yet, it did not happen quickly. Life moved on:

- They learned to **wait** on the promises of God.
- They learned that God could be **trusted** to do exactly what He said.
- They learned there was **nothing too hard** for God.
- They learned that in their **weakness**, He showed Himself **strong**.

- They learned that **they hadn't grown** as much as they thought they did – when
- Abraham lied to the prince of Gerar in the same way he had earlier lied to Pharaoh.
- They had a **long and full life** together. Neither was perfect – but they were both tied together and intertwined on every level of life.
- They knew each other's arms - the loves, joys, failures and pains... *and now Sarah was gone*...and Abraham was left – **a torn half of what once was comfortably whole. Abraham lost the love of his life...but he needed to keep going!**

Second, the <u>Lesson of Hyper-Sensitivity</u>: Loss will magnify existing feelings of weakness - so we need to work harder at trusting God in these times.

*Genesis 23:3 Then Abraham rose from before his dead, and spoke to the sons of Heth, saying, 4 "I am a **stranger** and a **sojourner** among you; give me a burial site among you that I may bury my dead out of my sight."*

Abraham recognized his position before those around him – they didn't feel as he felt, and didn't truly understand his perspective. He always knew he was an outsider, but now the intense loss heightened his sense of loneliness and made him feel like he stuck out on that hillside. He had God's promise that the land would be his children's land in the future... but for now he had title to nothing and was surrounded by strangers. He could easily have felt "no one had his back" – but that equation would have neglected to take into account the reality that **God's promises could be counted on**.

Loss will magnify weakness, but we must cling to God's promises in all times – and *especially* when weakened.

Third, the <u>Lesson of Clouded Values</u>: Loss can cloud our judgment to make unwise to remove a sense of burden – but we must be clear and careful to guard long term objectives.

*Genesis 23:5 The sons of Heth answered Abraham, saying to him, 6 "Hear us, my lord, you are a mighty prince among us; bury your dead in the choicest of our graves; none of us will refuse you his grave for burying your dead." 7 So Abraham rose and bowed to the people of the land, the sons of Heth. 8 And he spoke with them, saying, "If it is your wish for me to bury my dead out of my sight, hear me, and approach Ephron the son of Zohar for me, 9 that he may give me the cave of Machpelah which he owns, which is at the end of his field; for the **full price** let him give it to me in your presence for a burial site."*

Abraham heard (perhaps for the first time) the open respect and appreciation his neighbors had for his life and dealings with them. Look at the incredible relationship Abraham had with his unbelieving neighbors. They clearly had great respect for him (23:6); and he showed a great respect for them (23:7 and 12).

You need not give up the truth of God's promises to be respectful and caring to unbelievers! At the same time, Abraham did not want an unclear title to the land in which his family tomb would be established. He wanted to make good and clear decisions that would not create future troubles.

In pain, we can look for immediate fixes to our pain – but they must not come at the expense of long-term objectives.

A good decision is that which causes me to forfeit the immediate for the long term goal; a bad decision is one that causes me to forfeit a long term goal, for short term pleasure!

Abraham knew that paying now to clear the title before all men was better than taking a free option that would leave the future open to questions and problems. We can't throw overboard a lifetime's work to "make myself feel better" today.

Normally, counselors recommend to spouses to make no major changes in the first year after the loss of a spouse for that reason (if it can safely be postponed).

Broken and vulnerable, Abraham expressed both respect and thankful relief at their apparent honor – but he had a need that was very **time sensitive**. He needed – for the first time in his life – to **OWN a clear title** of **land** before those around him. God promised Abraham ownership of something that he now had to pay out of pocket for – because the promise of God was not yet realized.

Abraham had to be content to allow God to work later in what was already a firm promise. The lessons of his earlier life waiting for an heir for many years would now bear fruit as he surrendered the money and trusted that God would eventually live up to His promise. Abraham had learned earlier in life...**God may do some of what He promised us even long after we leave the Earth. He is under no obligation to meet our time schedules on things**..

Fourth, the <u>Lesson of Dulled Defenses</u>: Loss will make us vulnerable to some who will try to trick us – we must be careful to keep our eyes fully open without becoming jaded with everyone.

*Genesis 23:10 Now Ephron was sitting among the sons of Heth; and Ephron the Hittite answered Abraham in the hearing of the sons of Heth, even of all who went in at the gate of his city, saying, 11 "No, my lord, hear me; I give you the field, and I give you the cave that is in it. In the presence of the sons of my people I give it to you; bury your dead." 12 And Abraham bowed before the people of the land. 13 He spoke to Ephron in the hearing of the people of the land, saying, "If you will only please listen to me, I will give **the price of the field**; accept it from me that I may bury my dead there." 14 Then Ephron answered Abraham, saying to him, 15 "My lord, listen to me; **a piece of land worth four hundred shekels of silver**, what is that between me and you? So bury your dead." 16 Abraham listened to Ephron; and Abraham weighed out for Ephron the silver which he had named in the hearing of the sons of Heth, four hundred shekels of silver, commercial standard. 17 So Ephron's field, which was in Machpelah, which faced Mamre, the field and cave which was in it, and all the trees which were in the field, that were within all the confines of its border, were deeded over 18 to Abraham for a possession in the presence of the sons of Heth, before all who went in at the gate of his city.*

Abraham faced the harsh reality of life that even in his brokenness – others around him had their own agenda. They were not looking out for HIM. They were not FAMILY. This could only serve to *heighten his sense of loneliness* in the face of his loss. He may have suspected in the encounter that the open respect was not as genuine as it appeared on the surface. If he wondered, it **quickly became clear** the motives were not all genuine as the exorbitant price came out – but he was more concerned with avoiding shame. He told them to sell the land for the price it was worth. The average **cost of Hittite treaty purchases was four shekels an acre**, with fertile lands at forty shekels per acre. Ephron charged a great deal more for the land, but he lost something... his name. Note in the Hebrew of 23:16 the "vav" is missing in the copies of most texts. It is as though he *lost* his name in trying to *gain*! Since the cost was SO HIGH, why did no one speak up? Blood is thicker than water!

Fifth, the <u>Lesson of Lost Vision</u>: Loss can push us to lose perspective – we must not lose the bigger picture of what God is doing!

Genesis 23:19 After this, Abraham buried Sarah his wife in the cave of the field at Machpelah facing Mamre (that is, Hebron) in the land of Canaan. 20 So the field and the cave that is in it, were deeded over to Abraham for a burial site by the sons of Heth.

The burial of Sarah in this land under a permanent deed was an act of faith by Abraham. God had already told him that 400 years of captivity was coming (Genesis 15:13). Abraham looked past the obstacles to the promises of God! He learned to look long in the promises of God!

Look again at these lessons:

- **Unwarranted Futility:** Loss can make us want to give up – we must keep going for our whole journey here.

- **Hyper-Sensitivity:** Loss will magnify existing feelings of weakness - so we need to work harder at trusting God in these times.

- **Clouded Values:** Loss can cloud our judgment to make unwise choices to remove a sense of burden – but we must be clear and careful to guard long term objectives.

- **Dulled defenses:** Loss will make us vulnerable to tricksters – we must be careful to keep our eyes fully open without becoming jaded with everyone.

- **Lost vision:** Loss can push us to lose perspective – we must not lose the bigger picture of what God is doing!

Isn't it clear that loss in this life is part of God's training ground for all of us?

Reading the Map:
Lessons in Genesis

Lesson Twenty-four: Genesis 24
"A Family Affair"

There was a time not long ago that American life revolved around the FAMILY, not the INDIVIDUAL. Growing up, I recall the TV sitcom called "Family Affair" that aired on CBS from 1966 to 1971. Wikipedia adds: "The series explored the trials of well-to-do civil engineer and bachelor Bill Davis (Brian Keith) as he attempted to raise his brother's orphaned children in his luxury New York City apartment. Davis's traditional English "gentleman's gentleman," and Mr. Giles French (Sebastian Cabot) both had adjustments to make as he became saddled with the responsibility of caring for 15-year-old Cissy (Kathy Garver) and the 6-year-old twins, Jody (Johnny Whitaker) and Buffy (Anissa Jones)." The show was built on the idea of shared family responsibility, and that idea has now become foreign to many of us in American home life.

The Bible defines a family as a shared experience that is built on foundations God Himself has revealed. Today we want to uncover some of them.

Key Principle: God defines the family and God reveals how it should work.

Genesis 24:1 Now Abraham was old, advanced in age…

Family is about HONOR: Age is honored in a godly family. We cannot simply be about the NOW - that is an immature view of the world. Youth has vitality, but no chart to go by, no course to follow.

I am continually mystified at a culture that seems openly dismissive to those on whose shoulders we stand. The aging population seems obsessed with youth, in spite of their lack of experience and depth. I am continually amazed at how we FAIL

TO HONOR with words of encouragement and blessing those who have done so much!

In his autobiography, *Breaking Barriers*, syndicated columnist Carl Rowan tells about a teacher who greatly influenced his life. Rowan relates: Miss Thompson reached into her desk drawer and pulled out a piece of paper containing a quote attributed to Chicago architect Daniel Burnham. I listened intently as she read: "Make no little plans; they have no magic to stir men's blood and probably will not be realized. Make big plans, aim high in hope and work. Remember that our sons and grandsons are going to do things that would stagger us."

More than 30 years later, I gave a speech in which I said that Frances Thompson had given me a desperately needed belief in myself. A newspaper printed the story, and someone mailed the clipping to my beloved teacher. She wrote me: "You have no idea what that newspaper story meant to me. For years, I endured my brother's arguments that I had wasted my life, that I should have married and had a family. When I read that you gave me credit for helping to launch a marvelous career, I put the clipping in front of my brother. After he'd read it, I said, 'You see, I didn't really waste my life, did I?'" (Carl Rowan, *Breaking Barriers*, Little, Brown, Quoted in *Reader's Digest*, January 1992).

Let's be clear here, where honor has been earned, honor should be bestowed in a flood. God's desire is that we understand and honor our parents, those in authority, and those who have served before us. **We have attained no height without standing on their shoulders!**

*Genesis 24:1b ...and the **LORD had blessed** Abraham in every way.*

Family is about PATTERNS: These are established based on God's Word and what God has blessed. We look at what God has said and what God has blessed, instead of trying always to be the innovator. There is a place for innovation and morality is NOT it. Definition of family is NOT it.

Genesis 24:2 Abraham said to his servant, the oldest of his household, who had charge of all that he owned, "Please place your hand under my thigh..."

Family is about TRUST based on integrity, trust, and honesty that has been nurtured and demonstrated. Families must be able to trust that each member increasingly sees the need *to act with the other's best in mind. Selfishness is immaturity fleshed out. No family can survive* the excess of immature selfish thinking that opens the door to lies and deception. **When we decide that truth is not important, we open the door to a myriad of calamities.**

It reminds me of a story: A hiker was charged with eating an endangered species while tracking the woods of California. After hearing the man had eaten a condor, the judge quickly passed a harsh sentence of 10 years behind bars. The man pleaded with the judge to hear his side of the story because he felt circumstances justified his actions. The judge was interested to hear how anyone could rationalize killing a protected bird so he allowed the man to speak. The hiker explained how he had been lost in the wilderness for three days and nights without any food or water. He then spotted the bird sitting on a rock. With the little strength he had left, he threw a rock and killed the bird. After eating the condor he walked another three days without food or water before being rescued. He said, "Your honor, had I not eaten that bird, I wouldn't be here today." The judge was moved by the story and suspended the hiker's sentence. As they left the courtroom the judge asked the man what a condor tastes like. The man thought for a moment and said, "It's kind of a cross between a bald eagle and a spotted owl." (*Exec. Speechwriter*, V. 8.4)

*Genesis 24:3 "and I will make you **swear** by the LORD, the God of Heaven and the God of Earth, that you shall not take a wife for my son from the daughters of the Canaanites, among whom I live, 4 but you will go to my country and to my relatives, and take a wife for my son Isaac." 5 The servant said to him, "Suppose the woman is not willing to follow me to this land; should I take your son back to the land from where you came?" 6 Then Abraham said to him, "Beware that you do not take my son back there! 7 The LORD, the God of Heaven, who took me from my* *father's house and from the land of my birth, and who spoke to me and who swore to me, saying, 'To your descendants I will give this land,' He will send His angel before you, and you will take a wife for my son from there. 8 But if the woman is not willing to follow you, then you will be free from this my oath [to find him a wife at all]; only do not take my son back there." 9 So the servant placed his hand under the thigh of Abraham his master, and swore to him concerning this matter.*

Family is about CHOICES: These choices for the future are determined by God's promises and God's limits. When we decide to do what God has told us we may not – we endanger our families and our communities. The boundaries are set by God Himself. They come with great promises!

Genesis 24:10 Then the servant took ten camels from the camels of his master, and set out with a variety of good things of his master's in his hand; and he arose and went to Mesopotamia, to the city of Nahor. 11 He made the camels kneel down outside the city by the well of water at evening time, the time when women go out to draw water. 12 He said, "O LORD, the God of my master Abraham, please grant me success today, and show lovingkindness to my master Abraham. 13 Behold, I am standing by the spring, and the daughters of the men of the city are coming out to draw water; 14 now may it be that the girl to whom I say, 'Please let down your jar so that I may drink,' and who answers, 'Drink, and I will water your camels also'—may she be the one whom You have appointed for Your servant Isaac; and by this I will know that You have shown lovingkindness to my master."

Family is about DEPENDENCE ON GOD: Family success is bathed in prayer - for one another (24:12), specific and measurable (24:13), and met with active participation (24:14). We must work, but we must trust and pray. Note how this trait is displayed later in the story again:

Genesis 24:26 "...Then the man bowed low and worshiped the LORD. 27 He said, "Blessed be the LORD, the God of my master Abraham, who has not forsaken His lovingkindness and His truth toward my master; as for me, the LORD has guided me in the way to the house of my master's brothers."

Genesis 24:15 Before he had finished speaking, behold, Rebekah who was born to Bethuel the son of Milcah, the wife of Abraham's brother Nahor, came out with her jar on her shoulder. 16 The girl was very beautiful, a virgin, and no man had had relations with her; and she went down to the spring and filled her jar and came up.

Family is about VALUES: Establishing a solid home is based on the foundation of two people who are rooted in values: work (24:15) and chastity (24:16). Note the interconnection between the positive nature of her industriousness and the positive choices morally. If you are seeking a spouse - note it very carefully. Look for someone who is industrious about right things, and avoids wrong ones diligently. These values, displayed early, will be a great benefit in later years!

*Genesis 24:17 Then the servant ran to meet her, and said, "Please let me drink a little water from your jar." 18 She said, "Drink, my lord"; and she quickly lowered her jar to her hand, and gave him a drink. 19 Now when she had finished giving him a drink, she said, "**I will draw also for your camels until they have finished drinking**." 20 So she quickly emptied her jar into the trough, and ran back to the well to draw, and she drew for all his camels. 21 Meanwhile, the man was gazing at her in silence, to know whether the LORD had made his journey successful or not. 22 When the camels had finished drinking, the man took a gold ring weighing a half-shekel and two bracelets for her wrists weighing ten shekels in gold, 23 and said, "Whose daughter are you? Please tell me, is there room for us to lodge in your father's house?" 24 She said to him, "I am the daughter of Bethuel, the son of Milcah, whom she bore to Nahor." 25 Again she said to him, "**We have plenty of both straw and feed**, and room to lodge in."*

Family is about SERVICE: Two parents dedicated to serving Jesus by serving one another must work to raise children that understand the value of that service. Service takes sacrifice but reaps a loving bond. Rebekah was a woman of great strength and diligence - but all that was worthless without a heart to serve others.

Genesis 24:28 Then the girl ran and told her mother's household about these things. 29 Now Rebekah had a brother whose name was Laban; and Laban ran outside to the man at the spring. 30 When he saw the ring and the bracelets on his sister's wrists, and when he heard the words of Rebekah his sister, saying, "This is what the man said to me," he went to the man; and behold, he was standing by the camels at the spring.

Family is about COMMUNICATION: Communication is at the heart of family building. Sadly, because it takes time and sacrifice on the part of the hearer - it often gets put off. Children need to grow, and your constant input into their lives shapes the child.

Ed Stetzer, in an article about preaching, makes an interesting note: Sometimes, what they need is a universal translator.... It is much like what we need in a marriage relationship for spouses to understand one another. Let me give a few examples:

- When a husband says, "It's a guy thing," he really means, "There is no rational thought pattern connected with it, and you have no chance at all of making it logical."

- Of course, there is the cryptic statement, "I can't find it." Though difficult to understand, this means, "It didn't fall into my outstretched hands, so I'm completely clueless."

- Wives should take special note when a husband says, "It would take too long to explain." What he really means is, "I have no idea how it works."

Genesis 24:31 And he said, "Come in, blessed of the LORD! Why do you stand outside since I have prepared the house, and a place for the camels?" 32 So the man entered the house. Then Laban unloaded the camels, and he gave straw and feed to the camels, and water to wash his feet and the feet of the men who were with him.

Family is about HOSPITALITY: Healthy families know it is time to share with those who do not have what they have. All around us are hurting and broken people, and we can be Jesus to them. Nothing reaches someone like hospitality - food and fun together. It takes time and effort - but it yields warmth and friendship.

Genesis 24:33 But when food was set before him to eat, he said, "I will not eat until I have told my business." And he said, "Speak on." 34 So he said, "I am Abraham's servant. 35 The LORD has greatly blessed my master, so that he has become rich; and He has given him flocks and herds, and silver and gold, and servants and maids, and camels and donkeys. 36 Now Sarah, my master's wife, bore a son to my master in her old age, and he has given him all that he has. 37 My master made me swear, saying, 'You shall not take a wife for my son from the daughters of the Canaanites, in whose land I live; 38 but you shall go to my father's house and to my relatives, and take a wife for my son.' 39 I said to my master, 'Suppose the woman does not follow me.' 40 He said to me, 'The LORD, before whom I have walked, will send His angel with you to make your journey successful, and you will take a wife for my son from my relatives and from my father's house; 41 then you will be free from my oath, when you come to my relatives; and if they do not give her to you, you will be free from my oath.' 42 So I came today to the spring, and said, 'O LORD, the God of my master Abraham, if now You will make my journey on which I go successful; 43 behold, I am standing by the spring, and may it be that the maiden who comes out to draw, and to whom I say, "Please let me drink a little water from your jar"; 44 and she will say to me, "You drink, and I will draw for your camels also"; let her be the woman whom the LORD has appointed for my master's son.' 45 Before I had finished speaking in my heart, behold, Rebekah came out with her jar on her shoulder, and went down to the spring and drew, and I said to her, 'Please let me drink.' 46 She quickly lowered her jar from her shoulder, and said, 'Drink, and I will water your camels also'; so I drank, and she watered the camels also. 47 Then I asked her, and said, 'Whose daughter are you?' And she said, 'The daughter of Bethuel, Nahor's son, whom Milcah bore to him'; and I put the ring on her nose and the bracelets on her wrists. 48 And I bowed low and worshiped the LORD, and blessed the LORD, the God of my master Abraham, Who had guided me in the right way to take the daughter of my master's kinsman for his son. 49 So now if you are going to deal kindly and truly with my master, tell me; and if not, let me know, that I may turn to the right hand or the left."

Family is about TESTIMONY: The story is not just about what happened to us – but what GOD DID for us! We must share it to complete the work that God has mandated for us. Our family is a platform for ministry. When it is failing in some area, that platform is, for a time, damaged. Others will respond to what they see and hear when we have a story from the Lord to show in our families. It is not always a story of victory on victory – it can be a story filled with some dark times. The point of the story is not WHO WE ARE but rather WHAT GOD IS DOING in us - and that always ends well!

Genesis 24:50 Then Laban and Bethuel replied, "The matter comes from the LORD; so we cannot speak to you bad or good. 51 Here is Rebekah before you, take her and go, and let her be the wife of your master's son, as the LORD has spoken." 52 When Abraham's servant heard their words, he bowed himself to the ground before the LORD. 53 The servant brought out articles of silver and articles of gold, and garments, and gave them to Rebekah; he also gave precious things to her brother and to her mother. 54 Then he and the men who were with him ate and drank and spent the night. When they arose in the morning, he said, "Send me away to my master." 55 But her brother and her mother said, "Let the girl stay with us a few days, say ten; afterward she may go." 56 He said to them, "Do not delay me, since the LORD has prospered my way. Send me away that I may go to my master." 57 And they said, "We will call the girl and consult her wishes." 58 Then they called Rebekah and said to her, "Will you go with this man?" And she said, "I will go." 59 Thus they sent away their sister Rebekah and her nurse with Abraham's servant and his men. 60 They blessed Rebekah and said to her, "May you, our sister, become thousands of ten thousands, and may your descendants possess the gate of those who hate them." 61 Then Rebekah arose with her maids, and they mounted the camels and followed the man. So the servant took Rebekah and departed.

Family is about LAUNCHING: We are blessed to be a blessing. We are given so that can give. Our job is to protect, then prepare, then propel them into the exciting future God has for them. It can be a painful moment for a family - but it is part of the plan!

*Genesis 24:62 Now Isaac had come from going to **Beer-lahai-roi**; for he was living in the Negev. 63 Isaac went out to **meditate** in the field toward evening; and he lifted up his eyes and looked, and behold, camels were coming. 64 Rebekah lifted up her eyes, and when she saw Isaac she dismounted from the camel. 65 She said to the servant, "Who is that man walking in the field to meet us?" And the servant said, "He is my master." Then she took her veil and covered herself. 66 The servant told Isaac all the things that he had done. 67 Then Isaac brought her into his mother Sarah's tent, and he took Rebekah, and she became his wife, and he loved her; thus Isaac was comforted after his mother's death.*

Family is about CONNECTION: Depth of connection with God and with the others in the family brought consolation in the pain of loss, and the joy of intimacy in daily life.

When God wanted to change everything, He used a FAMILY.

One writer noted: "It was during the dark winter of 1864. At Petersburg, Virginia, the Confederate army of Robert E. Lee faced the Union divisions of General Ulysses S. Grant. The war was now three and a half years old and the glorious charge had long since given way to the muck and mud of trench warfare. Late one evening one of Lee's generals, Major General George Pickett, received word that his wife had given birth to a beautiful baby boy. Up and down the line the Southerners began building huge bonfires in celebration of the event. These fires did not go unnoticed in the Northern camps and soon a nervous Grant sent out a reconnaissance patrol to see what was going on. The scouts returned with the message that Pickett had had a son and these were celebratory fires. It so happened that Grant and Pickett had been contemporaries at West Point and knew one another well, so to honor the occasion Grant, too, ordered that bonfires should be built. What a peculiar night it was. For miles on both sides of the lines fires burned. No shots fired. No yelling back and forth. No war fought. Only light, celebrating the birth of a child. But it didn't last forever. Soon the fires burned down and once again the darkness took over. The darkness of the night and the darkness of war... (Sermon Central Illustrations, original source unknown)

That is how God reached the whole world. He used the message of the birth of a child to a young couple from Nazareth to light a lost and dark world... and He can use your family to share that light – if you will grab hold of the ROAD MAP for the family!

You see, **God defines the family and God reveals how it should work. He made it and He wants to work through it.** Families in our society are deeply in trouble, and that trouble has made its way into the church. We need **real transformation** in our families – and we all know it.

Mark Twain reportedly said, "The church is good people standing in front of good people teaching them to be good people."... but HE WAS WRONG.

That simply isn't true. We aren't trying to get you to **TURN OVER A NEW LEAF**; we are trying to **START YOU IN A NEW LIFE based on surrender to Jesus and His Word.** Old habits, old ways have to DIE and be supplanted by the NEW LIFE of Jesus in you.

Why isn't change occurring in all our families? Why is there a stalling effect that we are feeling in some? There are a number of reasons.

The fact is that TRANSFORMATION is a painful process.

- People are **stubborn.** (Have you ever tried to take something out of a two-year-old's hand?).
- People are **misinformed**. The fact is, there is a lot of misinformation out there about THE TRANSFORMATIVE EXPERIENCE of the Gospel.

I agree with Pastor Ed Stetzer's assessment: ...I am concerned when I hear someone boil the Christian experience down to praying a "sinner's prayer," and then being thrown back into the world to "just do it." When the "sinner's prayer" is the only definable moment of a Christian life, the Christian is robbed of so much more. (from my lecture notes).

Many people feel **trapped.**

Did you ever hear how to trap a monkey with a coconut? Hang a coconut from a string with a hole on the side. Put in something he wants. Make the hole large enough for the monkey to get his hand inside but too small to get it out without releasing the object he wants inside of it. He will hang there, caught, by his own refusal to let go of what he wants – even if it leads to his captivity.

We **are trapped by our own unwillingness to change our choices**.

- People are **blinded by comfort**. Some people keep a rotary phone, because they are comfortable with it. Others keep habits that are killing them, for the same reason.

- People are **afraid. Fear of the unknown is a primary reason people don't change**.

One speaker I heard said: "Some think following Jesus will make them a fanatic or, at the very least, socially awkward. The fact is - **change hurts for a time**. Start exercising and you will see that!" The problem is, God calls a believer to TRANSFORMATION - a transformed thought life, a transformed parenting experience, a transformed marriage.

The words of Thom Ranier help: "The alternative to this biblically mandated transformation is to pick a rut and make it deeper. He went on to say: The natural order of things is for energy to wane, and things come to a grinding halt. But the Christian life does not have that intention. God creates a new life in us and wants to transform our everyday living into a portrait of the gospel's power."

Get the power back on, and let the transformation continue. God made the family and He knows it can work when it runs on HIS POWER.

Reading the Map:
Lessons in Genesis

Lesson Twenty-five: Genesis 25
"Lessons from the Family Tree"

One of my favorite memories at Christmas time was a turning Christmas tree that my parents put up each year. It played music and turned the tree gently so that you could sit in the room at night and watch the colors of the tree lights as they produced ever-changing patterns on the walls and ceiling. During the day, observing the tree in the light yielded a whole different sensation. As it turned to display all of its bright decorations, you could see some of those were store bought, but many were hand crafts made by the dozens of children that grew up in our home. Since many were foster children that were with us for a time but did not remain for their whole childhood, items made by them recalled their time with us. Several hand-made decorations had small pictures that had been carefully placed on them from Christmases of our family's past. They contained faces of children that were now gone – perhaps now they looked nothing like that anymore. It was a *fascinating time to remember our shared family experiences*, and each of those children was very much alive in our memories.

In the "map book" of God in Genesis, the stories of the past were **told from a family album of tales and recollections** – not unlike what I remember in the pictures of that old spinning Christmas tree in my family's den. The faces brought back memories of long ago – but the lessons of their lives lived within us. The Divine Author shared His intent in offering the stories to us, as Romans 15:4 reminds: Everything that was written in the past was written to teach us. Genesis is a book "full of the seeds of things" - a book of beginnings - some good and some bad.

The book contains a road map of the moral and spiritual truths that men either <u>foolishly</u> <u>ignored</u> (to their destruction), or <u>wisely followed</u> (to their rescue).

Key Principle: The family was intended to be God's learning laboratory.

We learn our first lessons in the family – and all are *very* different. Even within a family we must understand that God has carved out very different paths for each of us. If you "freeze frame" on any family, a variety of lessons are being learned. Each member of the family is experiencing different lessons. God uses our family to offer us a place to learn the critical lessons of life.

In Genesis 25, we observe **six members** of a family in the short span of one chapter. Each was growing, changing – and facing the reality of life. Each was learning something different. For some, it was GROWTH toward knowing and loving God. For still others, they were learning how to deceive and cover – the results of which would show up in a later family album, or later reunion.

Families teach us that we cannot see it all at once. The one who looks successful this year may
look very much the opposite in five years. It is wise to take a longer view... For the next few minutes, let's consider this moment in time, long ago, and the lessons of one family that God was using to tell HIS story.

Abraham (Genesis 25:1-9) - Learning to move on in life to fullness.

*Genesis 25:1 Now Abraham **took another wife**, whose name was Keturah. 2 She bore to him Zimran and Jokshan and Medan and Midian and Ishbak and Shuah. 3 Jokshan became the father of Sheba and Dedan. And the sons of Dedan were Asshurim and Letushim and Leummim. 4 The sons of Midian were Ephah and Epher and Hanoch and Abida and Eldaah. All these were the sons of Keturah. 5 Now Abraham **gave all that he had to Isaac**; 6 but to the sons of his concubines, Abraham gave **gifts while he was still living**, and sent them away from his son Isaac eastward, to the land of the east. 7 These are all the years of Abraham's life that he lived, one hundred and seventy-five years. 8 Abraham breathed his last and died in a ripe old age,* *an **old man and satisfied with life**; and he was gathered to his people. 9 Then his sons Isaac and Ishmael buried him in the cave of Machpelah, in the field of Ephron the son of Zohar the Hittite, facing Mamre, 10 the field which Abraham purchased from the sons of Heth; there Abraham was buried with Sarah his wife.*

Two chapters ago we looked at how Abraham lost the love of his life and the companion that traveled the whole journey with him. She had ALWAYS been there in the story of his life's journey. He could not remember what life was like before SHE was in the picture. She was perhaps the key PLAYER in all the major movements and decisions he had ever made. Now she was gone. For many people that sounds like the END of their story. Yet, godly believers know that God isn't done with YOU when He recalls your partner.

He has more you must accomplish!

Abraham modeled this in his life. The passage helps us see **three truths about MOVING ON**:

a) **Abraham continued to intertwine his life with other people (Genesis 25:1-4)**. He took another wife. That doesn't mean that all of you in this situation need to do that – this was God's call on HIS life. At the same time, Genesis 25:1 reminds us that engaging others must be restarted. At the death of a spouse, it is natural to feel we must shut down. We weep and want to hide, as waves of grief crash over the jetty of our protected heart. We are broken. Yet, in time, we must open up and reach out anew. I don't want to be unfeeling in this illustration, but I want you to consider a great truth:

Both the hummingbird and the vulture fly over our nation's deserts. All vultures see is rotting meat, because that is what they look for. They thrive on that diet. But hummingbirds ignore the smelly flesh of dead animals. Instead, they look for the colorful blossoms of desert plants. The vultures live on what was. They live on the past. They fill themselves with what is dead and gone. But hummingbirds live on what is. They seek new life. They fill themselves with freshness and life. Each bird finds what it is looking for. We all do. (Steve Goodier, *Quote Magazine*, in *Reader's Digest*, May, 1990)

At some point, you must adjust your eyes to see the sweetness of life anew. Death is a part of life, but it must not replace the beauty of life. Abraham saw the joy of new life come from the tearing sorrow of death. He was learning to move on. Genesis 25:2-4 reminds us that full houses can snap us out of sorrow. For some of us, we just need to get busy and back into life.

Don't rush grief, but don't stay there. **There is more to life than your PAST – no matter how great that past was!**

b) Abraham attended to his legacy (25:5-7). He gave to Isaac what God told him to give, while giving generously to others to show them His values. Our legacy is best given while we can enjoy it! He gave to his family because he wanted them to know that he valued them and saw great promise in what God was going to do through them.

c) Abraham let people know that he was SATISFIED with life (25:8-10). They saw it. Do you suppose they could have known this if HE HADN'T SHOWN IT? Why is it that so many of us see aging as a penalty for life? I want to remind you that you are one day closer to death today than you were yesterday – and for a believer there is no sweeter reminder. **What awaits me is BETTER than what I have!** At the same time, I want to ask you – Are you communicating satisfaction with life or not? **Do people see your days as a bitter reminder or a better remainder?**

Isaac (25:11, 19-21) - Learning to trust God to provide as He did for his father.

*Genesis 25:11 It came about after the death of Abraham that **God blessed his son Isaac**; and Isaac **lived by Beer-lahai-roi**....19 Now these are the records of the generations of Isaac, Abraham's son: Abraham became the father of Isaac; 20 and Isaac was forty years old when **he took** Rebekah, the daughter of Bethuel the **Aramean**, to be his wife. 21 **Isaac prayed** to the LORD **on behalf of his wife**, because she was **barren**; and the LORD answered him, and Rebekah his wife conceived.*

There were three ways Isaac learned to trust God that offer a practical model to us:

Isaac recalled the provision and direction of God from the past (Genesis 25:11-19). Isaac was blessed by God, even as he had a walk WITH God. He went back to the place that took its name from the scene in Hagar's life, long before (recorded in Genesis 16) the first time she had run from Sarah. She was told to return and was given the promise of God's attention and provision for her son. Isaac chose to remain in that area. It may have seemed to some inhospitable, but to him it was a warm reminder.

The lesson is this: **When you need to trust God for your future, don't forget to look BACK and celebrate what God has done – it will build your confidence**!

Isaac recognized the need for separation to God for the promises of his future. (Genesis 25:20). God selected Abraham and openly pronounced Isaac as Abraham's inheritor. He told Abraham that in Isaac would be the line of blessing, and that line was to remain pure. Abraham went to great expense and lengths to be sure to follow his part on this. Isaac saw how Abraham treasured the purity of the line based on God's Word.

Here is a reminder: When God's Word marks boundaries in life – they are to be preserved. **We dare not seek God for greater provision while violating his Word.**

Isaac realized the truth of intimacy with God when troubles came (Genesis 25:21). Why pray? Because we need an intimate and personal relationship with God to stand up to the storms of life. Isaac knew that God could deliver in the need for a baby – because God did it for HIS DAD sixty years before. At the same time, he knew it took a relationship with God to steady him through the days of disappointment and keep him from undue impatience with God's timing!

Ishmael (Genesis 25:9,12-18) – Learning where he fit in the family as a unique man.

*Genesis 25: ...9 Then his sons **Isaac and Ishmael buried him** in the cave of Machpelah, in the field of Ephron the son of Zohar the Hittite, facing Mamre,... 12 Now these are the records of the generations of Ishmael, **Abraham's son**, whom Hagar the Egyptian, Sarah's maid, bore to Abraham; 13 and these are the names of the sons of Ishmael, by their names, in the order of their birth: Nebaioth, the firstborn of Ishmael, and Kedar and Adbeel and Mibsam 14 and Mishma and Dumah and Massa, 15 Hadad and Tema, Jetur, Naphish and Kedemah. 16 These Ishmael and these are their names, by their villages, and by their camps; **twelve princes according to their tribes**. 17 These are the years of the life of Ishmael, one hundred and thirty-seven years; and he breathed his last and died, and **was gathered to his people**. 18 They settled from Havilah to Shur which is east of Egypt as one goes toward Assyria; he settled in defiance of all his relatives (b'paney: in the presence of or before the face of).*

Ishmael learned to fit into the family in his unique place. He did it by:

a) **Taking responsibility for what was his to care for** (25:9). Ishmael lived with his father until he was sent away by Sarah when the boy was a young teen. He knew his dad loved him and he easily could have shut down completely when he was sent away. The division of the family was not a divorce, nor a rejection in the same way we would view the family today. It was a different time and Ishmael would have had different expectations than we would have today. At the same time, his feelings would have been as easily hurt as ours in the process. Yet, he knew when to come home – and he came back on the occasion of the burial of Abraham.

b) **Growing what was in his control instead of using his problems as an excuse** (25:12-16). He had many children, and became the father of chieftains that lived out in the desert camps, following the pattern of life their father carved out for them.

c) **Keeping himself connected to his family in spite of his uniqueness** (25:17-18). Ishmael was not like others, but that didn't mean he didn't need to be connected to them. He built a connection that came back to him at his death.

Rebekah (Genesis 25:22-24, 27b-28) – Learning to follow God in difficult times.

*Genesis 25:22 But the children struggled together within her; and she said, "If it is so, **why then am I this way?**" So **she went to inquire of the LORD**. 23 The **LORD said** to her, "Two nations are in your womb; and two peoples will be separated from your body; and **one people shall be stronger than the other;** and the **older shall serve the younger.**" 24 When her days to be delivered were fulfilled, behold, there were twins in her womb. ...27b Esau became a skillful hunter, a man of the field, but Jacob was a peaceful man, living in tents. 28 Now Isaac loved Esau, because he had a taste for game, but **Rebekah loved Jacob**.*

Rebekah learned to follow God in the turmoil and confusion of disappointment by:

a) **Dealing directly with God** (25:22). Rebekah suffered the stigma of barrenness for a time, and her husband prayed. She finally conceived and it was not a normal pregnancy. Complications began. The internal commotion within her womb became so severe that she wondered, "Am I am going to lose this baby?" So she said these words, "If it be so, why am I thus?" Or, "If the covenant of God is so, why am I having these problems with this pregnancy?" If I am in the will of God concerning this covenant, why am I having such severe complications? If God's word is so, why am I in this condition? So she began to inquire of the Lord.

God is not afraid of our questions. The Epistle of **James reminds us to ASK when we lack wisdom concerning trials.**

- There's not a storm so severe,
- There's not a trial so deep,
- There's not a mountain so high and,
- There's not a valley so wide,

- That God cannot conquer on your behalf!
- Be patient in your storm, for He will come walking on the water.
- Be patient in your fiery trial for He will walk with you through the flames.
- Be patient in your pain for He will give you a song in the night.

b) Accepting God's answer (25:23-24, 27-28). She simply believed that God had a purpose in the trouble because He said that He did. God wanted to show something about the lives of the two boys. She so believed it that she saw Jacob as the "special" one from the beginning. Sadly, she either did not understand what Jacob was becoming, or she participated in his manipulative ventures from the beginning, as she would at the death of her husband. Her alliance with Jacob became a serious problem – but that is a later story...

Esau (Genesis 25:25-34) - Learning what is truly important.

Genesis 25:25 Now the first came forth red (Lit: Admonee – ruddy), all over like a hairy garment; and they named him Esau (rough). 26 Afterward his brother came forth with his hand holding on to Esau's heel, so his name was called Jacob; and Isaac was sixty years old when she gave birth to them. 27 When the boys grew up, Esau became a skillful hunter, a man of the field, but Jacob was a peaceful man, living in tents. 28 Now Isaac loved Esau, because he had a taste for game, but Rebekah loved Jacob. 29 When Jacob had cooked stew, Esau came in from the field and he was famished; 30 and Esau said to Jacob, "Please let me have a swallow of that red stuff there, for I am famished." Therefore his name was called Edom. 31 But Jacob said, "First sell me your birthright." 32 Esau said, "Behold, I am about to die; so of what use then is the birthright to me?" 33 And Jacob said, "First swear to me"; so he swore to him, and sold his birthright to Jacob. 34 Then Jacob gave Esau bread and lentil stew; and he ate and drank, and rose and went on his way. Thus Esau despised (bawzaw: carelessly dispensed) his birthright.

The chief cause of failure and unhappiness is trading what you want most for what you want now. (Zig Ziglar)

There are three details about Esau revealed in the text:

- He was a rough child, different from most and more attached to the outdoors.

- He became a skillful hunter and formed an "earthy" attachment to pleasing his father in hunting.

- He did not learn until too late what was truly important. He treated his birthright as a   casual thing, and then deeply regretted it much later at his father's death.

It is the last one that requires a few comments. We must never forget that **spiritual blessings can be lost by living for the moment**. Note in 25:34 that Esau "*ate and drank, and rose and went his way.*"

He went on with life as usual, oblivious to the consequences of this one choice. The consequences of living for the moment were not immediate but they did come ultimately.

The birthright: given to the eldest son was his father's rank and position as the patriarch of the family or tribe. He became the leader at the death of the father and inherited a double portion of his father's property.

Hasty decisions usually lead to regrets.

What looked great and smelled sweet utterly deceived! Hebrews 12:15-16 warned: See to it that no one misses the grace of God and that no bitter root grows up to cause trouble and defile many. See that no one is sexually immoral, or is godless like Esau, who for a single meal sold his inheritance rights as the oldest son.

George Beverly Shea was once tempted to trade in some of the promises of God for a bowl of red stew. As you may know, George Beverly Shea grew up in a Christian household with

Christian parents. He was often encouraged to use his talents and his singing voice in the worship services of the Wesleyan Methodist churches which his father pastored. Finances were tight in the Shea household, so at 23 years of age, he had dropped out of college to work in an insurance office. He continued to sing in churches and on radio shows. Unexpectedly, George was one day called and asked to audition for a secular singing position in New York City. He passed the audition and was offered a substantial salary. While George was contemplating his decision, one Sunday, as he went to the family piano to prepare a song for the morning service, he found a poem that his mother had left lying around. She had been in the habit of leaving inspirational poems and lyrics around in hopes that God would use them to provide direction for George's life. As he read the lyrics of the poem, he was so profoundly impacted by the text that he immediately began to compose music for the lyrics, and used that song that same day in his father's church service.

"I'd Rather Have Jesus" became George Beverly Shea's theme song over the years. He says, "Over the years, I've not sung any song more than 'I'd Rather Have Jesus,' but I never tire of Mrs. Miller's heartfelt words." For George Beverly Shea, those words impacted him so deeply that he knew he must always give his talents and gifts to God, not ever trading in the promises of God simply for a bowl of red stew. (Osbeck, Kenneth W., *Amazing Grace-366 Inspiring Hymn Stories for Daily Devotions.* Kregel Publications : Grand Rapids 1990)

Don't forget that in Genesis 27:30-38 Esau's response as the reality of what he had done strikes home – but it was too late. Hebrews 12:17 further reminds us: For you know that even afterwards, when he desired to inherit the blessing, he was rejected, for he found no place for repentance, though he sought for it with tears.

Here is a warning, not only for the unbeliever but for professing Christians also: Be very careful not to despise the blessings and promises of God.

The day will come when consequences manifest themselves. In that time, your hardened heart and seared

conscience leave only bitter remorse. **Repentance is today's possibility. Don't wait!**

Jacob (Genesis 25:26-34) – Learning to manipulate people.

Genesis 25:26 Afterward his brother came forth with his hand holding on to Esau's heel, so his name was called Jacob; and Isaac was sixty years old when she gave birth to them. 27 When the boys grew up, Esau became a skillful hunter, a man of the field, but Jacob was a peaceful man, living in tents. 28 Now Isaac loved Esau, because he had a taste for game, but Rebekah loved Jacob. 29 When Jacob had cooked stew, Esau came in from the field and he was famished; 30 and Esau said to Jacob, "Please let me have a swallow of that red stuff there, for I am famished." Therefore his name was called Edom. 31 But Jacob said, "First sell me your birthright." 32 Esau said, "Behold, I am about to die; so of what use then is the birthright to me?" 33 And Jacob said, "First swear to me"; so he swore to him, and sold his birthright to Jacob. 34 Then Jacob gave Esau bread and lentil stew; and he ate and drank, and rose and went on his way. Thus Esau despised his birthright.

To really grasp Jacob's issues, we have to look later than this story to the deception he and his mother cooked up to get the blessing from Isaac. Imagine tricking your elderly, dying, mostly blind father – and having your mom help you do it! These two were a class act that day!

Look at the text and see three ways Jacob was set up as a manipulator:

- He knew from his birth his destiny – and that **privilege was assumed too early** in his life.

- He lived in a **comparative world where he was seen as the "good guy"** where his brother was seen as "an outsider". He hung out with his mom and was described as "perfect" (from "tamim" which may refer to his unblemished skin –   distinctly different from his ruddy brother).

- He learned the value of being clever over caring. He was ready for his hungry brother and he was prepared to get something from him in order to care for him.

The family was intended to be God's learning laboratory. Each member of the family is experiencing different lessons. God uses our family to offer us a place to learn the critical lessons of life.

Some learn the good things... The others – not so much!

Resources for Further Study

Books:

Cloud, Dr. Henry and Townsend, Dr. John. Boundaries, Grand Rapids, MI: Zondervan, 1992.

Groeschel, Craig. The Christian Atheist. Grand Rapids, MI: Zondervan, 2010.

Henry, Matthew. Concise Commentary on the Whole Bible. Nashville, TN: Thomas Nelson, 1997.

Lucado, Max. God Came Near, Nashville, TN: Thomas Nelson, 2004.

MacArthur, John. Found: God's Will. Colorado Springs, CO: David C. Cook, 2012.

Stroebel, Lee. The Case for Christ. Grand Rapids, MI: Zondervan, 1998.

Swindoll, Charles R. Stregthening Your Grip. Nashville, TN: Thomas Nelson, 2003.

Articles:

Brad Harrub, Ph.D., Bert Thompson, Ph.D., and Dave Miller, Ph.D. "The Origin of Language and Communication" (2003): Reprint from web at www.AnswersInGenesis.org.

McKeever, Joe. "Four Prayers that Changed My Life" (2014): From Sermon Central articles at www.sermoncentral.com.

Made in the USA
Columbia, SC
23 January 2024